BEHIND THE FACADE

Live Your Truth

A Hope Publishing Publication

www.behindthefacade.net

Carla Hope

Copyright © 2025 Carla Hope

All rights reserved. No part of this publication may be reproduced, distributed, or transmitted in any form or by any means, including photocopying, recording, or other electronic or mechanical methods, without the prior written permission of the publisher, except in the case of brief quotations embodied in critical reviews and certain other non-commercial uses permitted by copyright law.

Behind the Facade / Carla Hope
ISBN: 978-1-7642886-0-6 - Paperback
ISBN: 978-1-7642886-1-3 - E-Book
ISBN: 978-1-7642886-2-0 - Hardback
ISBN: 978-1-7642886-3-7 - Audio book

Dedication

To my daughters,

whose laughter is the melody in my quiet,

whose dreams are the stars I chase.

You are the ink in my pen,

the rhythm in my breath,

the story I never tire of telling.

May these pages carry whispers of my love,

and echoes of the wonder you bring to my world.

Live your truth.

Table of Contents

CHAPTER 1: Early Years 1

CHAPTER 2: The Lost Years 15

CHAPTER 3: Getting My Shit Together 36

CHAPTER 4: Marriage, Family, and the House 49

CHAPTER 5: The Trip that Redefined my Life 65

CHAPTER 6: Six Months of Hell 99

CHAPTER 7: Belonging 108

CHAPTER 8: Tornado 119

CHAPTER 9: Home 162

CHAPTER 10: The Physical Evolution 179

CHAPTER 11: The Argentinean Adventure 189

CHAPTER 12: The Stopover..................................... 215

CHAPTER 13: Thailand Tripping 230

CHAPTER 14: Battling the Black Dog 247

CHAPTER 15: Freedom 261

CHAPTER 16: The Story Goes On 272

ABOUT THE AUTHOR 277

Chapter 1

Early Years

---∞---

On the 22nd of April 1977, a baby, who was presumed male at birth, was born in Wollongong Hospital. As would become a trend in my life, I was born breech. Which meant the first thing the world really saw of me was my bum. So, things got off to a cracking start. The first few years of my life are a blur. The joys of being a newborn and not having a clue about what was going on around me! For the first few years, I lived with my parents in a flat in Unanderra near my grandparents' place. Both my mother and father worked, so I would get dropped off at my grandparents' home first thing in the morning and picked up later that evening. I guess these early interactions set the tone for my relationships. I was very close to both grandparents on my mother's side until they both passed away.

As I got older, my relationship with my grandparents grew quite strong, and I have fond memories of my time with them before starting school. Almost every Thursday, without fail, my grandmother would get dressed up, and we would catch the bus to the large shopping mall nearby. Whilst there, my grandmother would do a little shopping, but I always remember us having lunch at the Kmart cafeteria or I would get a meat slice from Guests Bakery. Once lunch was finished, and Nan had completed her shopping, we would catch the bus back to her home. Some days, we would walk back to Nan's home, which involved climbing what felt like a mountain to me. Other days, we would catch a cab, if she had too much shopping.

One of the funniest things I can recall from my time with Nan was when I lost one of my front teeth. We were sitting on the lounge together, and she was reading me one of the many golden books I had while I munched on my favourite biscuits, Honey Jumbles. Unfortunately, these soft ginger flavoured fingers were discontinued in 2021. But I digress… While munching on a biscuit, one of my front teeth came out. I remember my grandmother went into a bit of a panic and searched high and low for this tooth. She ended up concluding that I must have swallowed it, so we moved on and went back to reading the book again. What she later discovered, when she'd calmed down and was cleaning up, was my pearly white tooth firmly embedded in one of the Honey Jumbles. My grandmother also had a knack for getting me to go to sleep. Nan would lay me down and gently stroke my hair. This soothing experience still works on me to this day, but don't tell anyone.

My grandfather was a different kettle of fish. He was small in stature, built like a whippet but strong as an ox, and smoked like a chimney. The hard years of manual labour were etched on his skin and in his soul. I idolised him and used to follow him around like a puppy. He was always tinkering, building things from random parts, or pottering in his garden looking after his beloved orchard. I guess the tinkering came from his growing up on the farm at Eugowra in central west NSW. Like my grandmother, I have very fond memories of him. On one occasion, he was doing some concreting in the backyard, and I helped him. I walked through the trowel-finished concrete and drove my toy cars through it. Well, it was for the garage he was building! Apparently, my idea of helping was not appreciated as he chased me up the back stairs ranting and raving, bashing the shovel on the stair tread behind me. I got the hell out of there and ran to the safety of my grandmother inside.

My grandfather also liked a joke. When I was about five, I was taught to drive the tractor on the farm. I remember driving it one day across the paddock, and my grandfather threw something he had picked up off the ground at me. At first, I thought it was a stick but quickly realised that the stick was a snake. I bailed out of that tractor while it was still chugging along, now unmanned. While he thought it was hilarious, I sure as heck didn't. I think that moment solidified my dislike and fear of snakes that I still have today.

My father was not close to his family and as such, I have very few memories. I never got the chance to meet my grandmother as she passed away before I was born. My grandfather and two of my uncles lived in a government-owned home in Warilla. My most vivid memories of the home and then revolve around a wrecking yard. Both the backyard and the front yard were filled with old cars, boats, trailers, and just general junk. At least their house was always easy to find. I remember that inside the house wasn't much better, nor its occupants. Both my uncles were tall, large-built men who had let themselves go, to be polite. They had big scruffy beards, matted hair, would walk around with no shoes everywhere and dirty tatty clothes, even though they could afford new clean clothes. I always remember my dad commenting on how embarrassing they and the house were. It wasn't until I was much older that I found out why the rift existed between my father and his family. He was adopted with the family moving from England to Australia because of his health, a fact his stepbrothers resented.

When I was about two, we moved out of the flat in Unanderra into a home my parents had built together. Ironically, they purchased the land from someone who would come into my life some 14 years later. The house was large for its time—two-story, three-bedroom, brick home. Expansive glass windows that afforded views over the lake dominated the upper level of the front façade. The only downside was that every August we would get strong winds and sit nervously watching as the glass flexed under the strain of the wind gusts. I am amazed that they never failed. My room was at the front of the house overlooking the front yard and towards the lake. I spent many hours in that room as a child. Two large green garage doors dominated the lower story of the house. When opened, they revealed a cavernous space, which, at one stage, had 4 cars parked in there with room to spare. I am guessing this establishes my requirement for garage space wherever I live.

The backyard sloped steeply away from the home and was split into two sections. The front two-thirds was predominantly lawn, whereas the back third had vegetable garden beds. A passionfruit vine hedge split these two sections. This hedge was so large my mother hid a horse, which was a Christmas present for me, behind it for several weeks. As I got older, I used to sit out there picking and eating the fruit almost to the point of being sick. To this day, I still love fresh passionfruit. The grass area evolved over the years. When I was younger, it contained homemade climbing frames and obstacles for me to play on. As I got older, these were removed, and a large bird aviary took residence in the

Chapter 1

back corner. The aviary was full of budgies and quail. You would be woken early each morning to the sound of the birds. If I wasn't in my room, I was often outside entertaining myself in the yard by hitting or kicking a ball against the wall of the house. Occasionally, one of the neighbouring kids came over, and we played backyard cricket.

Lego was one of my biggest distractions during my early years. I would spend hours playing with the Lego that I had amassed. I guess it was really my first true obsession. My parents used to say that I knew every piece that I had. My Lego was stored in a compartmentalised box, just as I liked it. Sorted and organised in a way that worked for my brain. My Lego obsession ran deep to where I was entering building competitions by the age of 10. I remember Lego and Westfield shopping centres sponsored one of the first and largest contests I entered. They had set up a large table in the middle of the centre and gave us a few hours to free build something in line with the theme. I was fortunate as the theme was space, and at that point, I was building lots of spaceships and base stations. At the end of the build, all the models from the heat were judged, with the heat winner going on display at the shopping centre. I can still remember my build. It was a large ground-based space station complete with several rocket towers, rockets, spacecraft, and buggies. I had panels that opened and closed so the mini figures could get in and out of the station and the vehicles I had built. I was lucky enough to be selected as the heat winner. As I was in one of the first heats, it was several weeks until the overall winner was announced. I remember walking past my model and the new models thinking I had no chance. I was wrong. I won in my age group. The prize was cool, well, for a Lego child, anyway. It included several Lego kits and a trophy cup made of Lego. I kept this trophy for many years, but it disappeared a few years ago and hasn't been seen since. I have my suspicions about what happened to it but would never voice my thoughts.

Growing up, my mother was obsessed with horses. She used to keep one in a paddock down the road from the house. She would often check on the horse by standing in the front yard and whistling. Her horse would then reply. She would ride most weekends around the area. I guess at some point I may have shown interest, or she presumed, and I found myself the owner of my very own horse, Woodley Little Spider, a purebred Australian Pony. This was the horse that hid in plain sight in the backyard. Clearly my eyes were painted on, or I could never see beyond the fruit on the vine… Irrespective, I started joining mum on rides. We used to follow the power line easement from where the paddock was, over to the other side of Dapto and Lake Illawarra. We would regularly stop at a shop approximately halfway through the ride. This was a critical stop as we and the horses got ice cream. Yep, each of the horses got an ice cream tub, not that they were spoilt. Spider hung around for a few years until I started spending more time riding my bike around the streets. Something I could do whenever and on my own. Even at a young age, I liked 'me' time. I often wonder if this would have been different if I had had siblings. I guess that's a question that will never be answered.

The other thing that dominated my life in these early years was Scouts. I joined Second Dapto Scout Group at about the age of 7 as a Cub. From that point in time, Scouts Australia would become woven into my life story until my early 20s, so don't be surprised when the topic of Scouts reappears several times in the book. I have fond memories of my leaders and can still picture them today. One leader was a young, rotund, bearded man who was full of life. The other two leaders were a married couple. Unfortunately, the husband suffered from multiple sclerosis, and I recall his health declining over the years until he could no longer be an active leader in the group. I still used to see him around after he left Scouts as he was the local police Sargent. It was during this time that my inherent nature to push myself to achieve, or try to overachieve, showed through. Within the first 18 months of being there, I had progressed through the various award levels available. Most nights, I would present to the leaders several projects or activities that qualified me to earn a badge. It got to where my uniform sleeves were full, and I could no longer fit all the badges on my shirt. Now that I am older, I reflect on this and think that this characteristic was fuelled by my underlying lack of self-confidence, something I still struggle with today.

From the outside, people would look at my early years as being blessed. Truth be told, my world was far from perfect; in many regards, it was the complete opposite. I grew up in a dysfunctional house where my parents lived under the same roof but had very separate lives. The house alternated between silence and all-out war. My dad lived at work, and when he would come home, he would either go to his bedroom or to the garage and tinker with his car. My mum would do the same. If she was not at the school where she taught, she was in her study doing schoolwork. This was never a home; it was a house occupied by three people. As I grew older, I learned how dysfunctional the family was.

My primary education was at Stella Maris Catholic Primary School in Shellharbour, half an hour from where I lived. Why was I there? The answer was convenience. My mother taught there, so getting to and from school was easy. This had advantages and disadvantages. I don't know which one was stronger. On the way to school each morning, I would be drilled on spelling and times tables. The plus side was I knew my spelling words and times tables each week; the downside was there was no downtime. One of the biggest advantages was what I call lunchtime specials. My mother would regularly take me to the local bakery or fish and chip shop. I was often the envy of the other kids. This was a double-edged sword as I would often be isolated because of this. I would also be at school very early and leave late because of my mother's commitments. This made my school days very long. The school was nowhere near where I lived, so I had no local friends, and my friendship base from the school was limited as I couldn't spend time with them.

My mother used to go away on overnight excursions with the class that she taught. This meant that I would stay with one of the other teachers from the school. I would stay with her as my father lived at work, and I had no one to look after me or get me to and from school. I used to think the world of her. She was a single, young lady who lived near Oak Flats High School. Mum would take me to school, and I would go home with her, where I would stay for the few nights that my mother was away. One of my strongest memories goes back to when I was in about Year 2, and I had her as a teacher. She was always dressed very femininely, in stockings, skirts, and the like. I remember I used to sit near her when she would read stories, and I would stroke her stocking-covered legs. This is a feeling I will always remember. As time went on and

I got older, I remember at different times stroking her legs when I would stay at her place, but she would encourage me to slide my hand further up her leg and eventually it got to the point where I was not only stroking her stocking covered legs but also her vagina. In time, I remember helping her get dressed for a heritage day at the school. I was too young to realise what was going on back then, but today it makes my skin crawl. In hindsight, this was my first sexual experience at the age of about nine. I hope and pray that I was the only one ever exposed to this.

At Stella Maris, there used to be several telegraph poles laid on the ground for sitting and playing on. When I was in year 4, I was playing with friends, and one of the poles dislodged, rolling onto my leg, crushing my ankle. Eventually, a few of the teachers rolled it off my ankle and helped me up. As I could walk, nothing was thought of it. Not long after, I found that my ankle would collapse. My mother found out about the incident and took me to the doctor. It was discovered that the telegraph pole had damaged my ankle, which required surgery. As expected of a 10-year-old, I was terrified. I remember at one stage telling my parents that I was going to kill myself before I had surgery. A slightly extreme and illogical option, I know, but I was a panicked kid and just wanted it all to end. A few weeks after the accident, a local surgeon, who tried a new reconstruction technique out on me, operated. While the surgery may have gone according to plan, the damage done to my ankle still causes me issues today. The recovery and current issues may have also been exacerbated when I fell down about 6 steps early in the recovery phase. Ironically, the same teacher who concealed the initial injury failed to inform my parents about my falling down the stairs. I was also to blame, as I used to just suck it up and move on, saying nothing, no matter how hurt I was. A character trait I often deploy today to my detriment.

During the primary years, my mother used to take me to her friend's place every Friday night. I would also spend most weekends there and even take trips to Sydney, where her mother lived. While there, we would often bake biscuits and cakes. Maybe this is where I got my love of baking from? She was a single mum and had a son a few years younger than me. To be honest, we never really got on. It was more of an exercise in tolerance. In time, my mother packed up and left my father, moving in with her. I had no idea what was going on. One day, I was living on Thirroul Road and the next, in a small house in Berkeley. I was lost. What I had thought was a family was now ripped apart. Eventually, my mother moved us back to Thirroul Road. She claims she moved back because I was not coping with the separation and being away from the family home. Despite moving back to Thirroul Road, the regular Friday, and weekend visits continued. Little did I know that my mother was a lesbian. A fact I would only realise when I was much older. It was at this point I realised why the household was so dysfunctional.

In 1987, I was 10, and my mother took long-service leave. We headed off on a trip into Central Australia for 10 weeks. Accompanying us were her partner and her son. This was not the first trip I had been on with Mum as we had been to various parts of Victoria. These trips were never a family thing. As she was not comfortable travelling on remote dirt roads, most of the trip was spent on sealed roads. We still got to see a lot of places in western Queensland, the Northern Territory, South Australia, and Victoria. This trip opened my eyes to how magical Australia is, making me fall in love with the remote areas. Looking back, I have lots of positive memories and recognise how lucky I was to see so much of Australia at the age I did.

Following the trip, I became increasingly involved with Scouts and in solo activities such as riding. I was so distracted that I didn't realise my mother had distanced herself from her partner and grown closer to other women. As I look back with what I now know, the relationship was breaking down, and my mother had explored relationships with others.

1988 was my last year of primary school. While the year was relatively uneventful, life at home continued to be dysfunctional. To distract myself from the reality of my world, I continued to invest a lot of time in Scouting, taking every opportunity possible to be out of the home. I also spent a lot more time going for longer road rides on my own. The solitude of riding was comforting; it gave me time to think and forget about the world that was. That year saw something unusual happen; my father took me away for a week to Queensland. Over the week, we went to the World Expo and theme parks. I think this was the longest time I have ever spent one on one with him. I still cry today over the fact that growing up and even to today, I really didn't know my father.

Chapter 2

The Lost Years

―――――∞―――――

In the late 80s, I started at St Joseph's High School as most of my primary school friends went there. After the first year, I, along with my best friend, became the target of bullying from that so-called group of friends. The bullying towards me was targeted at me being gay, a fag, to use their words. While I felt uncomfortable in my skin, I had mentioned nothing. Maybe I just gave out signals I was different; I didn't fit the stereotype of your typical teenage boy. In hindsight, I didn't. The first signs of gender dysphoria were showing, but I never recognised them as that. It was during this time that I started drinking in secret. It was my escape from the reality of school life and the tumultuous home life.

Now that I am taking the time to stop and reflect on life, I realise that I have been lying to myself for so long. When I was about 12, I remember going to Coles and buying a couple of Valentine's Day packs that they had. The packs contained a lace bodysuit and matching stockings. I hid those under the drawer under my bed. My mother found them one day, and she sat me down and told me it was ok to be gay, but if I was a cross dresser, a drag queen, or whatever, she would take me to get counselling, as that's just sick. Love the Catholic extremist. I guess hearing that from your mother is one way to shut you down and repress yourself. A few years later, I started working at a local chemist. While I worked there, I bought makeup and stockings. Again, these were found, and I was told again by my mother that I was sick. This is a pattern that would repeat itself for many years. I would find various places to hide things, and she would somehow find them, including a stash in the ceiling void.

At the end of Year 8, my mate had left and went to Edmund Rice. With him moving schools, my support network was no more, and the bullying intensified to the point where I would do everything I could not to be at school. Midway through Year 9, I transferred to Edmund Rice and reconnected with him. My time at Edmund Rice was interesting. I was in a school where I was more accepted, and bullying did not occur. But the feelings of discomfort about who I was remained. The skinsuit didn't match the way I felt. I had teachers who encouraged me to grow academically even though they knew I was just floating my way through school. I did also arrive at a time of controversy, as the child abuse scandal that involved several of the brothers and local priests had hit the media. While this did not directly affect me, in later life, I found out that I had confided in one priest involved in the abuse as he was the school's counsellor. I had discussed at length with him what had occurred to me in my childhood. In discovering this, I felt violated, but I felt comforted as I knew he was going to spend the rest of his life behind bars.

In Year 9, I met my first love. She went to Saint Marys and was a friend of some girls I went to primary school with. After meeting at a school disco, we then caught up the following weekend and started dating shortly thereafter. It was a very intense relationship where we both wanted to be with each other all the time. Within the first month of dating, we had slept together. I guess this was my first consensual sexual experience. I will never forget the conversation we had a few days later when she thought she was pregnant. As a 14-year-old, that scared me. Fortunately, she was not, and it did not slow our sex life down. She would do roller skating for school sport and once finished, would walk to my home, which was just up the road. As we were always home alone, we would end up sleeping together. This was a weekly event. On Saturdays, we would meet at a friend's place and catch up with the bigger group. Sundays were usually spent at her place, where we would spend the day in her room. During this time, my dysphoria was less intense, but I still had a niggling discomfort that I continued to tell myself was because of the abuse.

Chapter 2

This relationship went on for over two years. I can't explain why we split up to this day. Maybe it was because I had drunk heavier than I had in the past and distanced myself. When we split up, we didn't see each other at all. I was surprised when I got a call, and she asked me to go to her Year 12 formal. I agreed, and it was a great night. We reconnected that night and spent ages talking. Our second attempt at having a relationship only lasted a short time. I lost contact with her and do not know where she is today, but I still think about her and wonder what she is up to.

During my time at Edmund Rice, I attended a Christian boy's camp run by a local priest. My mother thought that going to the camp would help me meet boys of similar ages who were already at Edmund Rice. We all got on a ratty old bus and headed off to various locations around the state. I remember we stayed in Cooma for a few days. On one of those days, we hiked from Charlotte Pass to Mt Kosciusko and back. This is a long hike, and it was hot and humid. During the hike, I got chafing between my legs and buttocks. Despite the discomfort, I pushed on. Later that night, we were taken to the pool at Cooma, where we showered. Back in the day, the shower was simply a row of shower heads hanging off the wall, zero privacy. The priest walked up and down the row whilst we all showered. I felt him hovering near me, and then he made a comment about the chafing looking quite bad. For him to have been able to see the chafing he was having a good look. He told me at that point he had some cream that could help settle it down and could put some on when we got back to where we were staying. I said thanks but no thanks, as I have my cream. Later in the trip, we were camping near the Big Hole outside of Braidwood on the Shoalhaven River. The priest came and asked me to go for a walk with him and chat about the bullying, among other things. As we got out of sight of the main group, he tried to place his arm around me. This did not overjoy me, and I pushed him away. In pushing him away, he stumbled and fell to the ground. At that point, I told him never to touch me or talk to me and stormed off. I told nobody about this for years.

One of my most interesting memories from my time at Edmund Rice was in Year 10. My English teacher was a bit of an oddball and, to be honest, I thought he was a creep. He had a habit of sitting on the corner of your desk when he would talk to you. He did not do it to everyone, but he did it to me. I had asked him many times not to do this, as I found it uncomfortable, yet he continued to do so. Well, that all ended with a bang. On that day, he sat on my desk and started talking to the class. I had had enough by this stage and flipped the desk, which made him fall, and I went off at him. As I walked out of the room, I grabbed the door and head-butted it. That was where the issue started as the door was a solid core door and had a sheet of glass in it. I had head-butted the door so hard that I cracked it and then put my head through the glass. As the drops of blood rolled down my face from the cut above my eye, I walked back in calmly and packed up my bag and then left. I headed to the office and told them what had happened, and that I needed to get some stitches. One would expect that a student doing something like that at a Catholic boy's school would cause suspension or expulsion. Instead, the school apologised for what went on, and the teacher did not return to the school after the term break. I think the school may have learnt their lesson.

As I approached 15 years of age, I started trying to work out what was next in Scouting as 2nd Dapto did not have a Venturer section. One of the new cub leaders decided she would try to set up a section. It was at this time I met a group of people who would be part of my life for only a few short years but had a significant impact on it, and not in a good way. As with the other sections of Scouts, I was driven to achieve the highest award possible. I did this in 1994 when I achieved my Queen Scout Award. As the group was not overly keen on doing outdoor activities, I did not get out and do too many adventurous things. In fact, most weekends comprised the group gathering at one of the girls' places and drinking themselves silly. By the time I turned 16, I could happily drink a case of beer or a bottle of spirits and still be able to function. Much of this year was a blur because of my drinking habits. I attended the National Venture in Queensland. As part of the Venture, I spent a few days camped on Great Keppel Island, where I went diving for the first time. I should also note that it was one of the most spectacular places to drink yourself to sleep at night. But I did have a rude wake-up call courtesy of the incoming tide one night.

When I was 15, my parents brought me my first car. It was a 1966 XP Falcon. The car was silver blue and had been converted to a V8. Not long after owning the car, it was stripped with a view to repainting it and putting it back on the road. But as would become a trend in my life, the simple repaint became a rebuild with more modifications completed. I guess my feeling of not being enough manifested in the things that I owned; specifically; they were not good enough either. Unfortunately, the panel beater who was engaged to do the bodywork and repaint the car took several years to do the work. Eventually, I took the position of the freshly painted hot pink Falcon. By the time the bodywork was completed, I had lost interest in building the car, and it sat half-finished for several years. At one stage, I splurged and bolted most of it back together, but I never finished it. The Falcon was sold in 2002 and stripped by the new owner. My first car never saw the road again.

In 1993, I told my parents that I wanted to drop out of high school as I simply did not want to be there. I had decided that I was going to go to TAFE and try to get an apprenticeship. My mother was not happy with this and wanted to talk to a few of my teachers and see what they thought. After an extended period, I could leave and started completing a mechanical pre-apprenticeship course at Wollongong TAFE. Towards the end of the course, I was offered a job with Cleary Brothers as an apprentice plant and heavy vehicle mechanic. I was over the moon as I had proven to my parents that my decision to leave was not a bad one. Unfortunately, on the day I was due to sign my indenture papers, I was walking across some rocks when they moved, resulting in me breaking my ankle. My boss at the time was an arsehole and made me work for another three hours before we left on the hour-long drive home. That injury resulted in my having surgery and eventually having to leave Cleary Brothers in 1997, as I could no longer stand on my ankle for extended periods of time.

After leaving Cleary Brothers, I drifted from job to job and couch to couch for a few years as I was a bit of a lost soul. The dysphoria during this period was quite intense, and I would satisfy it by buying various items of clothing that I would wear in private. These moments would make me feel at peace but disgusted with myself. I would typically bin things regularly, not realising I was denying my true self and the fact that I was transgender and dealing with gender dysphoria.

Not long after leaving school, one of the local priests, Morrie, called me up and asked to have a chat with me. I had a lot of respect for Morrie. He was a former teacher, professional boxer and had served in the military. Morrie was covered in tattoos and missing most of his teeth. He was a real and genuine man who had lived a life before becoming a priest. It was during this meeting that I disclosed what had happened at the camp. He also told me he was helping the local police, who were conducting investigations into priests. Based on this, I ended up having to supply a statement to the police. I was crushed at the end when they told me they could not charge him because I had stopped him from conducting an act of indecency. This advice still makes my blood boil today. Unfortunately, the priest's uncle, who was the bishop, used his influence to get the priest out of the country. Eventually, the priest who tried to assault me was charged but got off on the charges. The saddest part of the story is that, crushed by the events and the backlash from local priests for bringing these issues to light, Morrie ultimately took his own life. He hung himself in the gym he built to teach kids boxing in on March 26, 1998. I will forever miss Morrie. He is a genuine hero to me and many others.

Chapter 2

While I thought I had put the attempted assault and Morrie's passing behind me, in 2013, it was all brought back up with the Royal Commission into Institutional Responses to Child Sexual Abuse. As part of the investigation, I had one commissioner contact me and ask if I was prepared to tell my story to them. Following the first contact, a teleconference was arranged. Over two and a half hours I retold my story and the impact that it had had on my life. I discussed not only what went on at the camp, but what occurred at Edmund Rice, and when I was a child. By the time I hung up, I was emotionally drained and unable to focus. After taking part in the meeting, I heard nothing more from the Commission. I often wondered what had happened to the information I had provided to them. It felt like years, but I eventually had time to review the Commission's final report and was glad that they had listened, not only to myself, but to all the others who told comparable stories.

Throughout my late teens and into my early 20s, I would hide in the gym. It was not uncommon for me to spend around four hours a day training. All this training resulted in my consuming massive amounts of food. A chicken washed down with a 1kg tub of yogurt was a snack. I had to feed the beast. No matter how large or strong I got, I was never satisfied. I could be bigger, I could be stronger, in fact I will be. It was at this point in my life that I started contemplating the use of steroids. My first exposure to them was through work, where one of the other mechanics said he could get me some. I accepted the offer and purchased the ampules and got the needles and syringes I needed. But I couldn't do it; I couldn't inject myself, so I hid them in the garage. This was a move I would live to regret as my mother found them, and all hell broke loose. After this incident settled down, I again felt the urge to try steroids. This time, my supplier was a known steroid junkie from the gym I trained at. This guy was a man mountain but with twigs for legs. He was so out of proportion that it was funny. Irrespective, he could get me what I wanted. This time, it was to be pills, nice and easy, but I knew they were more damaging to my kidneys and liver. After using up the first bottle of pills, I ordered another. This time, the order didn't go to plan as my supplier thought he would swap out the tablets for vitamins. I called him out on this, and it didn't go down too well with him. Calling him out triggered a roid rage. He punched me in the nose, breaking it, and tried to strangle me. Following this experience, I recognised I didn't need steroids. To be truthful, I was stronger than my supplier and almost as large as him, but with well-developed legs. In hindsight, my gym obsession was about building my façade. I was protecting myself from being hurt. I was also subconsciously hiding the truth, the real me.

Chapter 2

When I was 17, the chaotic world that I lived in completely fell apart. My father announced one day that he had left. He'd had enough and wanted to restart his life. I was angry and upset but now realise the importance of being himself and being happy. Not long after moving out, he got on a plane and flew to England. I didn't know it, but he had met someone over there and had been planning to move and live with her for some time. It was around this time that I suffered my injury at work. It was on the day of my surgery that he flew out of my life to establish a life with a new family overseas. It was the day my already patchy relationship with my father completely imploded. A few years later, he flew back and announced he was here to stay as his relationship had ended in the UK. But within a month, he was gone again. He flew back out of my life, only returning to Australia when I turned 21. To this day, I don't really have any relationship with him. While I sit here and type these words, I do not know if he is even still alive.

Not long after my father moved out, my mother's new partner, a woman, moved into Thirroul Rd. As I was already dealing with my father leaving and battling my own demons, this really threw a spanner in the works. The frequency and intensity of arguments between my mother, her partner and me increased rapidly. There were several times when various objects, such as heavy drinking glasses, were thrown at me. I no longer felt as though I had a safe place. It was during this time that I did a lot of couch surfing or stayed at various partners' homes. Things continued to decline, and I moved out of the house with no desire to ever return. This period in my life severely damaged my relationship with my mother. At best, my relationship with her would be described as distant and, to a degree, cold. This relationship has never recovered, and probably never will, to how it was prior to this time.

At 18, I started training to be a cub leader with 2nd Dapto. Not long after this, I was introduced to the 4th Wollongong Rover Crew and transferred groups. At the same time as transferring groups, I trained to be a Scout leader. It was during this time that two amazing ladies entered my life. Their children were involved in the Scout group. These two took me by the hand and helped me survive the next few years. They offered me a place to rest my head at night when I could not sleep in my bed. They held my heart when I was lost. They inflated my tyres when I was flat. I spent many weekends at their home. Sharing a drink, sharing a laugh. They were and always will be, my other mothers. These two saved my life. I think I would have ended it all if it weren't for them. I don't think they will ever truly know how important they are and how much I love them.

Chapter 2

Joining 4th Wollongong was a wonderful experience. Most weekends, I would have my car packed, and a few others and I would be off somewhere camping, hiking or canyoning. Those years were some of the best years of my life. My obsession with achieving awards remained, and I achieved the Baden-Powell Award in 2000. In January 2000, four friends and I from the Rover crew headed to the South Island of New Zealand for a month. That trip was amazing! We did so many things while we were there. We travelled by train across the island via Arthur's Pass and then headed to Fox Glacier, where we went ice climbing. That was a wonderful experience until I put a crampon spike into my calf. It hurt a lot, but it did not stop me. When we arrived at Queenstown, we did all the typical activities, such as jet boating and rafting. A couple of us even went downhill mountain biking. It was in Queenstown that I got my eyebrow pierced. Several hikes, including the Routeburn, Kepler, and Milford tracks, followed Queenstown. As always, I somehow ended up skinny dipping, but this time it was in Lake Te Anau, a deep and cold glacial lake. Other highlights for me included staying overnight in Mueller Hut above the cloud line near Mt Cook. The view was breathtaking.

Unfortunately, that trip changed my relationship with two people on the trip. While we were away, two of the guys frustrated me for different reasons. One of them couldn't make a decision to save his life, which did my head in. The other was just lazy and would not help when we had to do group activities such as the pre-hike food shopping. Those relationships never recovered.

When I turned 18, I started working in security to top up my income and to stop myself from drinking myself stupid most nights. Working the pub doors is a real eye-opener. I was fortunate as I had a regular Friday night placement at a pub in Kiama called Tories. I also had a regular partner who understood how to read me and interpret what was about to happen. This pub was quite a tranquil place to work, as regulars who mostly behaved frequented it. But there were a few who would be barred regularly. One of my funniest memories was when one lady bit me on the arm and then tried to have the police charge me with assault. I think what made my time enjoyable was that after I finished work, I would often go back to my mate's house, and we would eat a packet of Tim Tams and drink a bottle of scotch.

My Saturday nights were a bit more dynamic while I was based at the Harp in Wollongong. I would often end up having to go to Waves to help manage the issues that occurred there as it approached closing time. I have so many glorious memories of the Harp. Prior to the renovations, the karaoke stage was placed where it overlooked every corner of the pub. I would spend most of my time standing there. I remember the lady who ran the karaoke saying to me that it was great having me on the stage as they knew exactly what was going on. She told me I had a behavioural pattern. Apparently, I used to progressively take earrings out, chains and watch off and place them on one of their speakers. They knew that if I got to the point of all jewellery being off; I was getting ready to jump in and break up a situation. She also told me that after I had dealt with whatever had gone on, I would put all the jewellery back on and behave like nothing had happened. At the end of every shift, we would have staff drinks until the early hours of the morning. We would also often head across the road to the cocktail bar and keep drinking there.

You may hear people make comments about security staff being renowned for one-night stands. I can neither confirm nor deny this. What I can confirm is I do not know how many partners I had during that stage of my life. I think my longest relationship I had during these years was only a month. Even during these longer relationships, I would often be unfaithful, sleeping with different girls most nights. It is not something that I am proud of when I look back on it now. I think it was all about trying to build and maintain a hyper-masculine façade. But I was not happy and struggling to fight the black dog; my mental health was not good.

By the time I got to the age of 21, my life was a fair mess. I had lost my way and was just surviving and going through the motions. To be fair, if it were not for my other mothers, I think I would have been dead. All I really had in my life that had any meaning was my involvement in Scouts. To make ends meet, I was working at Civic Video as a deterrent to potential thieves and as security in pubs several nights a week. These two jobs made me enough money to survive, but just.

My mother insisted that I have a 21st birthday party. I told her I did not want one and that if I had one; I would not remember it. The party was held at the 4th Wollongong Scout hall and attended mainly by family and friends from Scouts. My other mothers were there as well, even though my mother hated them. Not that she had met them. My memory of the party is very vague. From what I have been told, I had already drunk over half a case of beer before people arrived. I think what finished me was drinking a yard glass filled with Cointreau. I have very vague memories of ending up at the Harp. I was told when I started my shift the following week that the bar staff were giving me quick fuck shooters (Midori, Kahlua, and Baileys Irish Cream) in spirits glasses rather than shot glasses. No wonder I can't remember anything. The next morning, I woke up at an ex-girlfriend's place in her spare room. I do not know how I got there, but I am still thankful to this day that she looked after me, as the amount of alcohol I had consumed probably came close to giving me alcohol poisoning. I was still over the limit three days later.

One thing that I have always been able to do is completely zone out of everything around me. On my actual birthday, I was at one of my other mother's places and was drowning my sorrows. I was told by one of her sons that I sat down with a paper clip and used it to grind 21 lines in my right thigh. I have no recollection of doing this at all, but I do have 21 scars, so I guess it happened. It was not long after this that I decided I needed to try to get my shit together.

In my early 20s, I built myself a Hilux 4WD. The ute was set up for serious off-road work, camping and to be used in long-distance rally racing. This thing ended up being a hybrid of parts. About the only unmodified genuine Toyota part left was the shell. The ute had an engine and transmission from a supercharged Monaro, differentials from a Patrol and custom-built suspension. Once completed, the ute was capable of speeds over 200km/h and still articulated so that I could place diagonal wheels on 44-gallon drums and the other two remained on the ground. This was my toy.

While a member of Rovers, I again ended up becoming involved in the leadership side of things. Over the four years, I went from being the Regional Chair, to two years as the

State Chair and a year as the National Chair of the respective Rover Councils and a member of the Scouts Australia National Executive. It was during this time that my love of Scouts changed. In 2002, it was agreed that Rovers NSW would sponsor my race truck for a season. As part of the arrangements, we offered two seats in the ute for the Kidney Foundation rally to the highest fundraisers in the section. But as no one fundraised, we did not fill the seats. It was not long after I got appointed to the national role that the new incoming State Chair accused me of committing fraud. After many exchanges of correspondence, which highlighted that I had signed none of the cheques, and none were made out to me, the correspondence ceased, but my love for Scouts was destroyed. I ended up resigning from the national position mid-term and turning my back on Scouts.

Throughout my late teens and into my 20s, James was one of my best mates. I first met him when I went to the 4th Wollongong Scout Group. He was one of the Venturers. He also lived next door to one of my other mothers. He was a funny character and would say and do some odd things that would make you laugh. James worked as a locksmith in the family business. He was obsessed with locks and exceptionally skilled. Whenever I needed locks changed or installed, he would do it for me. James was also an active member of the Australian Defence Force (ADF) Army Cadets. As the years passed, our friendship grew. He became my younger brother from another mother.

Chapter 2

While I did not get to catch up with James as often as I liked, we stayed connected. On August 24, 2003, I was returning home from a medical appointment when I got a call from my partner telling me I needed to come to her office. When I arrived, she greeted me. It was at this point that one of my other friends came in and told me that James had passed away that morning. I was told that his parents found him in his room. His cause of death was unknown at the time and subject to an inquiry. I still don't know the exact cause of his death to this day. But in reality, it doesn't matter as he was gone. I was absolutely devastated and did not know what to think, do or say. As I am sitting here writing this, I feel the tears building up, something that happens whenever I think about losing him.

That afternoon, we gathered at my other mother's house, which, ironically, was next door to where James lived. I did not realise how much was involved in organising a funeral at that stage of my life. I can remember meeting along with his parents, with funeral directors, compiling photos, building slide shows, and for me, writing his eulogy. That was one of the hardest things I have ever had to write in my life. To this day, I do not remember if what I said on that day did him justice and represented how much he meant to so many of us. James was a Ford nut like me. In planning his wake, I approached the local Ford dealer to see if I could buy one of the enormous flags they flew at the dealership. I was pleasantly surprised when the dealer principal brought out a brand new one and said Take it; it's yours. I still have that flag to this day and cannot imagine ever parting with it. Many of the drivers he used to admire have since signed the flag. It is among my prized possessions.

I was a mess on the morning of his funeral but somehow held it together. My hyper-masculine façade helped me do this. I remember carrying James' coffin into the church and placing it on the stand. As he was a member of the ADF, the coffin was draped in an Australian flag and had a beautiful floral arrangement on it. In my pocket, I had my fourth Wollongong scarf, a scarf, which meant so much to the both of us. As I gave his eulogy, I hung onto that scarf. I do not know what it was, but hanging onto it enabled me to keep my composure. It was not until I sat back down that I broke down. It was dawning on me he was physically gone. Following the church service and the placing of his casket into the stretched Falcon wagon, a select few went to the crematorium for a private service. To this day, I can still visualise his casket going through a wall of blue flames as it was transferred to the cremator.

James' ashes now live at Mt Keira Scout Camp near the fire circle. While I know they are there, I could never go to his last resting place. James, I know you are up there looking down. I hope you know I miss you, my friend, and I will see you on the other side.

Chapter 3

Getting My Shit Together

By the time the late 90s rolled around, I had completely lost the plot. It was like I was adrift at sea with a broken rudder, no navigation system and a broken engine. The black dog was biting hard. Episodes of self-harming had increased in frequency, and my drinking had become heavier. Ironically, I don't know if it was the drunken haze or my ability to separate my mind and body, but I was oblivious to the harm I was doing to myself and the impact my spiralling had on others. I needed to wake up and get my act together before I ended up with nothing and no one in my life.

In 1998, I got sick of floating aimlessly through life and believed I could be more than I was. But I did not know how I was going to do this. I had no HSC, no trade, and I had no other qualifications. During one of my more lucid moments, I thought about going to university to study something and possibly have a career. While I did not know about the logistics regarding how this idea would come to fruition, I raised it with the other mothers. After a bit of research, the other mothers and I identified a road. The University of Wollongong (UOW) had just introduced a pathways program through the UOW College. After downloading the forms and compiling the information required, I spent a few nervous weeks waiting to see if I would be accepted into the program. I will always remember the day when the letter arrived. I was in! I had an opportunity to potentially get myself into university and start heading in the right direction. I was committed and ready to study. I needed to hit the reset button.

The first day of the program was spent in a common room going through the logistics of the program. The course covered a range of subjects, such as Maths, English, and History. By that stage, I thought that engineering would be what I would like to do. I felt it would help me establish a good career path and be something I would enjoy. It was during this time that I was handed a piece of paper, which showed the marks you needed to get to get into various degrees. Wow! I needed to achieve an average mark of 87% to get into engineering. My heart sank as I didn't think I had any chance of obtaining that mark. Here I was, a high school dropout, who when at school, had just floated through. How on earth would I do this? Even though I thought I couldn't achieve that mark, my ASD tunnel vision and need to overachieve kicked in. I needed to prove to myself and the surrounding others that I could do it. I could and would succeed. Over the semester, I worked my butt off. Every spare moment was spent working on assignments or studying. This hard work paid off as at the end of the semester, my weighted average mark across the subjects was in the mid-90s. I was in! I could technically enrol in any degree offered at UOW. I had just proven to myself that I was not a dumb dropout. I could excel when I put my mind to it. Despite the achievement, the voices in the back of my head overprinted these messages and told me it was still not enough, and I had fluked my way in.

With my access program certificate and mark in hand, I filled in the paperwork and enrolled in environmental engineering. My application was accepted. I was officially a university student. No longer an underachieving high school dropout. I thought that the next four years of my life were mapped out. To my surprise, I got a call from the dean of engineering requesting a meeting. I thought to myself, why does the dean of engineering want to meet with me? Not long into the meeting, after all the pleasantries were done, I found out what it was about. I was not welcome in engineering. The Dean said to me, "I don't know how you got here, but you will fail within the first semester; you don't belong here". As the conversation went on, his primary concern was my ability to complete the math courses. Wow, what a way to encourage a new student! I was crushed to hear these words, but I went, no, bugger you. I will prove to you what I can do. He had just waved a red flag in the face of a raging bull.

In 1999, I started my engineering degree at UOW. As I was still working part-time, I took on only three subjects. I was enrolled in maths, a design subject, and a computer subject focussed on engineering drawing. I will admit it was a shock to the system. I really struggled with the maths as it had been so long since I had dropped out of school. Irrespective, I pushed on, and I passed the subject, which I was happy with. I really enjoyed the design subject as we worked on a project that was judged by the academics. My group designed a new hopper for powder feeding. I was amazed, and we made it to the finals. While we didn't win first prize, I thought it was a significant achievement, nonetheless. The drawing subject was an interesting one. While I was happy to work with the pencil and paper, I struggled with the computer programming side of things. At that point in my life, I had not even owned a computer, let alone done any programming. I remember doing the first test, and the lecturer came up to me and said, "I thought you were a lot smarter than that, fat boy". My blood boiled, but I didn't respond. It just made me more determined to push on. After the second test, which I just passed, he made a similar comment. This time, he followed up his initial comment with, "So, you're not a fat boy, you're a hitman." He was referring to the fact that I had my security uniform on as I had to start work straight after the tutorial. I lost it. I got up from the computer I was working on and walked him against the wall. I told him he needed to be very careful with what he said next as I had had enough of his comments. At that point, he backed down and apologised. I went and packed my stuff up and left. The next day, the head of the subject, Ernest, asked me to see him to talk about what had happened. Following our conversation, Ernest taught me the content one on one. It was through his help that I ended up getting a significant mark in the subject. This was a rough start and soured my university experience. At the end of the first session, I took the next session off. I had run out of money and was a little disheartened. Maybe engineering wasn't for me?

Towards the end of 1999, my enthusiasm and drive to make something of myself returned. It didn't take me long to recognise that science is where I should focus my attention. I enrolled in a Bachelor of Environmental Science to begin session 1 the following year. I was really looking forward to going back and trying again. I was determined that 'take two' would be a success. I would overcome the financial struggles I faced the year before, and I felt more confident in the fact I could succeed. A meeting with the sub-dean, Adrian, bolstered this confidence. Adrian was a funny character who reminded me of Papa Smurf. His face and beard, aside from being dark, were just like the characters. Behind the beard, he wore a warm and welcoming smile; he was full of life and would become a mentor to me as the years went on.

In 2000, I began studying three subjects to enable me to earn just enough money to survive from week to week. Two of my three subjects were Earth Science-based subjects. One was Igneous and Metamorphic Rocks, and the other was a Physical Geography subject. I loved both subjects and was encouraged to succeed by the academics who taught them. This encouragement sparked my deep-seated interest in the Earth Sciences and made me want to learn more. I had found my happy place; I was going to follow my passion for once. I again completed three subjects in the second semester as this balance appeared to work for me. I had accepted that the three-year degree would end up taking four years, but at least I could do it. In the second session, one subject was Sedimentology-based. It was at this time that a truly amazing man entered my life. Brian could best be described as a hyperactive whippet. The man was everywhere; he was a ball of knowledge, a brilliant communicator and, most of all, had so much time for the students, including me. I was pleasantly surprised when, at the end of first year, I received some academic awards in Earth Sciences I was hooked, particularly on sediments. Brian's passion underpinned this love. It drew me in. Over the following years, I formed a strong relationship with Brian and shared so many significant memories. He holds a special place in my heart and became the first male that I felt truly believed in me. He wanted me to succeed and grow. If it were not for him, I would not be the person I am today — a debt that I can never repay.

One of my fondest undergraduate memories revolves around a trip to central Australia in 2001. I was in an interesting position on the trip, as not only was I a student but also the trip mechanic. Skills I needed to call on several times during the trip. Although it was not intended, I ended up doing quite a lot of driving the university's ute and towing one trailer. The first day of the trip was a long day, made longer by the fact I was fixing one trailer only a few 100km from home. As I was driving into town, I could feel the trailer tracking poorly behind the ute. On further inspection, I discovered that the trailer's wheel studs were smaller than the holes in the wheel. This had resulted in three of the five shearing off and the other two well on their way to doing the same. As we were in Bathurst, I could reach out to one of my good friends who helped me find the parts I needed to fix the trailer before heading off. We still had a long drive ahead and pulled into Burke close to midnight. I was beat, and it was only day one. By this stage, I had already worked out it was going to be an interesting trip.

The trip covered some familiar territory as we worked our way through Queensland to the site of the dig tree. We spent one night at this location, but in the morning, we took scenic flights over the Cooper Creek floodplains. The pattern on the ground was simply spectacular. We then spent a few days at Cullyamurra Waterhole and explored around Innamincka. During one of our exercises where we were collecting samples, our recovery rate was low, so one of my group members urinated down the hole. He wondered why no one had wanted to touch the samples after that. Brian was renowned for grabbing his swag and heading off away from the group to sleep each night. One night, a few of the students got drunk and accidentally ran over him as they went screaming through the bush. A few other interesting things happened while we were there as one bus started playing up. I remember getting a call over the radio from one academic saying he had no power, so he had taken the air filter out of the bus. Not a great idea on the dusty central Australian roads. After a while, I narrowed it down to a fuel issue. The problem was that the filter was jammed on, and the spare had a different part number. It took nearly a day to get confirmation that it was a suitable replacement. Once confirmed, I had to destroy the old one to get it off, but we were back up and running once I got it changed.

Another highlight of the trip included walking across Lake Eyre and sinking to my knees in the mud while Brian stood next to me and laughed. My return to the lake in 2021 was slightly less eventful, but nonetheless impactful in my life. Given the trip had been going for a while, a few of the PhD students had niggled at each other. I remember getting a shovel and digging two sizeable holes in the bank's side we were looking at; it was a calming experience. Each hole was the perfect size to drop a body in, ironically. I now look back and laugh about it, but I was not laughing at that time.

Some of the mechanical mayhem that occurred on this trip kept me on my toes. On our way to Marree in South Australia, one bus was driven through a washout at speed. The biggest issue was that the washout was deep, with steep entries and exits. Hitting the washout forced the bus's radiator back into the fan, which cut a massive hole in the radiator. The driver was oblivious to the carnage they had caused until about 20 minutes later, when the bus overheated. After crawling under the bus to identify the damage, I was shocked we had gotten as far as we had up the road. I could see daylight through the radiator core. When I crawled out and informed Brian of the damage, one of the other academics suggested I should solder it. He was a true academic — very intelligent, just no common sense. To amuse myself, I got the academic to look through the front of the bus as I put my hand through the radiator and grabbed his. This shocked him but made him realise the seriousness of the issue. We ended up towing the bus over 200km to the township of Copley, where a new radiator was flown into town a few days later.

In 2004, Brian offered me an honours project looking at how the Wandandian Creek Delta had formed. I loved going in the field with Brian; we just worked so well together. I couldn't believe how much we could achieve in a short time. We worked so well as a team; it was like we could read each other and predict what was next. With Brian's support and encouragement, I achieved first class honours. The research was also published in the Australian Journal of Earth Sciences. The high school dropout had achieved something that people didn't think I could.

However, this was not the end of the journey as my relationship with Brian continued to grow, and I ended up doing a PhD under his guidance. The PhD extended the work I had completed in my honours. But this time, I was taking on two larger deltas and trying to understand their responses to sea level change and anthropogenic modifications to the surrounding environment. The first 18 months of the PhD had me busily core drilling on land and collecting samples in Lake Illawarra. In April 2007, life threw a curveball, and I took up a job opportunity at the local council. Taking up this role complicated things from the perspective of completing the PhD. With Brian by my side, I pushed on and submitted my thesis towards the end of 2012. I remember Brian sitting with me one night and breaking the news that the markers were not satisfied with the PhD and wanted it to be rewritten. I was absolutely gutted and didn't want to know about it anymore. Like so many other times in my life, I was ready to walk away. Brian didn't let me do this. He coached me, and I resubmitted the thesis. This time, the thesis was passed. In 2013, I graduated and was now a doctor... Who would have thought!

While at UOW, I was fortunate enough to become involved in the delivery of subjects. I held several positions over the years, ranging from demonstrator through to subject coordinator. I used to love taking students on field trips. I would have to say that the 10 days in Eden each year was the one I loved the most. I still miss doing this trip today. As with my studies, Brian would be by my side throughout this phase of my life. I loved this experience, as it allowed me to share my passion with others. It was the highlight of my time at UOW. Deep down; I had always hoped that I would make a difference to at least one of the students' lives, and they would remember me down the track. I was pleasantly surprised when a few of my old students started at Council and remembered me and what I had taught them. I guess I had achieved what I had hoped I would.

During my time at the university, I formed some strong relationships with the academic and professional staff. The strongest of these was with Brian, as mentioned, as we worked well together in so many ways. Brian, to me, was more than a mentor from an academic scene. I looked at Brian as a male role model, something I missed in my life. I am so grateful that Brian entered my life, and we have remained close to this day. Korin was my Brian equivalent from the professional staff. I would spend hours talking with them about so many things, but mostly about how I could make my ideas come to life using Geographic Information System (GIS) software. After leaving UOW, I lost contact with Korin. On March 31, 2022, an email was circulated about Transgender Day of Remembrance (TDOR). I was surprised to see who the email was signed off by. It took me a while to realise what I had read and immediately felt the need to tell Korin about myself. My email read, "*I just read your email that you sent around yesterday. Happy TDOR. While it's not common knowledge, it was my first.*" This initial email started an email exchange that lasted for hours. As part of the email exchange, Korin commented, "*I guess we know why you and I have always gotten on so well.*" Clearly, our intuitions were telling us something that we were not ready to hear.

When I started the PhD, I also started studying a Graduate Diploma of Education through Charles Sturt

University. In hindsight, I now look back and wonder what I was thinking taking that on, on top of the PhD and the teaching that I was doing. Irrespective, I pushed on. Although I pushed on, I nearly didn't finish it because I started at Council. The only reason I could finish it was because of the support of one of the senior managers, who enabled me to take the leave I needed. By the end of 2008, I had successfully completed the diploma and graduated.

To this day, I have a thirst for knowledge and have completed a variety of courses covering topics such as carbon accounting, project management, green buildings, climate risk, and asset management. I believe I will never stop learning and growing — a belief that Brian instilled in me over the past 20 years.

Chapter 4

Marriage, Family, and the House

―――――∞―――――

It was late in 2000 that I met Ares at a mutual friend's place. She was not the typical person with whom I would have a relationship, but something was different about her. Over the next few weeks, we got to know each other better. I even helped her paint the townhouse she had just bought. Not long after meeting, we moved in and started our life together.

When we met, Ares worked at KPMG Chartered Accountants. She had established herself as a tax expert and was on her way to developing a successful career. In contrast, I was lost. I had no career and was just trying to get my shit together while finishing up my first year of uni. She took me in and supported me, given I couldn't contribute much financially. Instead, I took on the role of doing a large amount of the maintenance work around the complex and our townhouse. Over the years, I built retaining walls and letter boxes, removed trees, built a garden shed and landscaped the complex. Life was good, but not perfect. She would remind me continuously that it was her home, and I didn't contribute

Chapter 4

to it. I guess, therefore, I always felt it was a house, not a home. Irrespective of everything, I still felt strongly about her.

Her family welcomed me with open arms. Her mum, dad, and sister are all beautiful people. Prior to going to Christmas that year, I was taught two Hungarian phrases. The first was 'nem vagyok éhes' and the second was 'nem cur parlinco'. I was told they were two important phrases that I needed to know. The first translates roughly to 'I'm not hungry' and the second was to say, 'No thank you to alcohol.' Not long after getting to her parents' place, her father handed me a glass full to the brim with whiskey. It was only 8 am... That glass followed me around all day until I drank it. The biggest issue was that I didn't like whiskey. I hadn't drunk it since I finished the cradle of Johnny Walker in three consecutive nights. While her father was asking me about alcohol, her mother was constantly trying to get me to eat. It was at this time I realised why she had taught me the phrases she had.

Over the next few years, our relationship progressed. Mostly, things were good. So good, in fact, that in 2002, we started talking about getting engaged. But this came with its own challenges. She declared she wanted to pick the stone and her ring. I guess it was only logical, given she would wear it. My biggest concern was paying for it, as I knew she would want something impressive and high quality. She deserved it, but I couldn't afford it. The hunt for a stone began with the jeweller bringing in several stones. Eventually, she found one that she liked, and we purchased it jointly. After a few more weeks, and many designs, the ring was finished. During this time, she decided I should also wear a ring. When the jewellers went to size my finger, they had to use a cable tie as the ring sizing tools were not large enough. Both rings were put away until I proposed to her. Something I did that Christmas. I placed the ring in a Swarovski crystal ring box and wrapped it up as one of her presents. It was a special day; I had met the person I thought I was going to spend the rest of my life with, and she wanted to share her life with me.

Not long after getting engaged, our attention turned to the wedding. As she came from a European background, the wedding was always going to be an enormous affair with extended family and friends. After a brief search, we found a venue and locked in the date.

A few months out from the wedding, she threw a curveball at me. She declared that I needed to sign a prenuptial agreement before the wedding could go ahead. This request rocked me. It felt like she was setting the marriage up for failure even before it began. It was ironic as the prenup was not worth the paper it was written on, from a legal standpoint, and she knew it. This declaration resulted in a tumultuous period. The suggestion hurt me — that all I wanted was to get my hands on her money and property. Eventually, I agreed to sign the document as I was committed to marrying her. I was also cognisant of the amount of money that we and our parents had already invested in the wedding. For the rest of our time together, it was to be her way or the highway.

February 5, 2005, is a day I will always remember. It was the day that I married the person I thought I would spend the rest of my life with. We were married in a beautiful old sandstone church on the hill overlooking Jamberoo, a small country town. That morning, myself, my groomsmen and father-in-law met at the church and erected a flower arch over the doorway. Inside, one of the local ladies had put stunning floral arrangements together for the ceremony. The church looked amazing. I was really looking forward to the day. A few hours later, the boys and I headed to the church in my heavily modified Hilux 4WD. All suited up, we waited for her and the rest of the bridal party. As with most times, she turned up late. The priest was not overly happy about how late she was. Irrespective of the circumstances, the ceremony went according to plan. The priest was a well-regarded singer, and he ended up singing much of the ceremony. This made it even more special. Following the ceremony, we headed for a rural property, which had panoramic views of Kiama and the coastal plain, for photos.

As expected, we had a large and over the top reception. The night got off with a bang. We entered the reception to the symphony version of Metallica's Nothing Else Matters between two walls of fireworks. The rest of the night was a choreographed blur. The reception had been planned to within an inch of its life. I remember when it was being organised; her parents were focussed on the food and alcohol side of things. We ended up having a 7-course meal, and the alcohol flowed freely. No one that night went home hungry or thirsty, I can assure you of that. At the conclusion of the reception, we spent our first night as a married couple at a rural getaway.

We spent the following day at her parents' home. Traditionally, Hungarian weddings would be celebrated for days. This was our compromise. We spent the day eating and drinking with family and friends who called in. This was a great day where we got to relax and celebrate the wedding. A few days later, we flew out for our Hawaiian honeymoon.

Hawaii was unlike any of our previous holidays. We didn't stop. It was go, go, go. Mostly, Hawaii brings only fond memories. I still laugh at the Americans who said to us they just wanted to listen to us talk as they loved our accent. I had no idea what they were on about given I thought we sounded similar. It wasn't until we heard another Australian that we understood how different we sounded. While there, we did so many amazing things, such as parasailing and going to see the Pro Bowl, the all-star American football game. On the way to the Pro Bowl game, I felt someone poking me in the back. When I turned around, there was an American couple smiling back at me. His first words were, *"Sorry, just trying to work out if that was you or you had shoulder pads on."* I cracked up laughing and told him it was all me.

After our two weeks in Waikiki, we headed to Kauai, another smaller and less developed island. Whilst there, we again didn't slow down much with almost every day filled with trips. One highlight for us was a happy hour with unlimited Mai Tai cocktails. By the end of the week, I had progressed to drinking on average 12 in an hour. Life was grand, well, until the night before we were due to fly home. That night is a mystery to me as I have very little recollection of what went on. All I know is I had only had a few drinks, and I was out of it. Apparently, I couldn't talk or walk straight. At dinner, I couldn't hold a knife or fork. I was a space cadet. Later that night, I apparently passed out in the bathroom. I was right royally in trouble with her, but I had drunk little. I had drunk a spiked drink. The ramifications of that drink meant we flew home a day later than originally planned and had a $15,000 USD hospital bill. All I can say is thank goodness for travel insurance.

In 2007, my world changed. It was the year I found out I was to become a parent for the first time. I was elated to know that in 9 months, I was to be a father. This was a time of great joy in my life. Both of us appeared to be in a good place and were focussed on trying to provide a good environment for the new bub. I was asked regularly if I cared what sex the baby would be and, to be honest, I didn't. But when I found out we were having a little girl, I was over the moon. I would have a beautiful little princess in my world. Throughout the pregnancy, all I prayed for was that my little girl was healthy and would live a happy life.

On April 8, 2008, Bel joined our family. This was one of the happiest days of my life. Witnessing her birth and cutting the umbilical cord are etched in my mind. She was perfect. My heart was hers from that moment in time. I declared I would move heaven and earth to give her the life that she deserved. I didn't want her to grow up experiencing some things I experienced. I wanted her to grow up in a home full of love and happiness, not a house at war.

We thought we were well prepared for her arrival. But one thing we had forgotten, or not even thought about, was mittens. Bel had sharp claw-like nails and would constantly scratch her face. I was on a mission to protect her from herself and headed to the shops to get mittens. I found mittens and about a dozen little outfits. I couldn't resist; they were cute. I liken my experience to going grocery shopping when you're hungry. You buy everything and anything that catches your eye, often not buying what you needed to get. It took several shops and several more outfit purchases, but I eventually found mittens. Triumphantly, I returned to the hospital to share my success. I had conquered the world of baby clothes shopping, and her face would be safe from her claws. Keeping mittens on her hands was nearly as impossible as keeping an ecstatic father from excessive buying of baby clothes.

The day came when we were to take Bel home. But overnight, her skin colour shifted, and she took on a shade of yellow. Following some tests, she was transferred into a humidity crib to treat the jaundice. It was hard to see my baby girl wrapped up in the crib, but I knew it was for the best. Fortunately, it was only a little over 24 hours, and she was cleared to go home. Carrying her out of the hospital and placing her in the car seat was an amazing feeling. It became real. I was now responsible for her life.

The first year of her life was uneventful. She hit all her milestones and was a happy baby. I was still over the moon. Her mother spent the first six months with her at home watching her grow. I had hoped to take parental leave, but we were in the middle of a restructure, and I didn't feel safe taking leave. To this day, I rue missing out on this opportunity. I was jealous of her and have always felt like I missed out. During this time, my relationship with Bel's mum was relatively stable, as we were both in a good place.

Over the next few years, we went about life as a happy family of three living in the townhouse at Blackbutt. But as Bel grew, we both felt the need to buy or build a family home. We initially bought the house next door to Ares' parents' place, intending to knock down the old house and build a new one. But the banks didn't like that idea and would not release the finances needed to build. We decided to put the property on the market and try to find somewhere else to buy and build. Our search led us to Shell Cove and a block that hadn't been registered yet, and after some back and forth, we ended up buying the block. This was a challenge as it was the second-highest price paid for land in Shell Cove and the financial crash. Persistence paid off, and the block was ours. This block was almost perfect. It was a large corner block, relatively flat and overlooking the State Park. We could build what we wanted and never be built out.

The building process was painful at best. Once I drew the house, Ares had one of the building companies she had worked with provide us with a tender. I was reluctant to go with them given they couldn't even get the tender right. Yet she insisted we build with them. I expected the build would be challenging, and I was correct. The first issue we came across was that the slab was formed and poured in the wrong spot. This meant that the retaining walls and other elements like the water tanks would not fit, triggering a redesign and new DA. The challenges didn't stop there. Every day was a recent issue. One of the largest issues related to the roof. The tilers paid no attention when laying the terracotta shingles, resulting in the roof looking like the rolling swell on the ocean. The issue was so severe; it had to be escalated to the national product manager, who came to the site and stood with a laser pointer highlighting to the tilers every tile that needed to be replaced. It was ridiculous. The build timeframe blew out, which meant we had to move in with the in-laws. By the time the build was completed, Fair Trading had issued an order for the rectification of 56 defects.

A few months into the construction phase of the new house, Ares announced she was pregnant with our second child. As with most things in our lives, the pregnancy and preparations were tightly project managed. All that was missing was the Gantt chart showing the elements and critical path… While I was elated that we were going to become parents again, this time felt different. I was a lot more relaxed about it, as we had done this already. We can do it again; I was not wedded to the Gantt chart. I just wanted us to enjoy the time. Over the next 9 months, we prepared for the birth of our second daughter. I felt that the relationship between us was at its best when she was pregnant.

Like with Bel, she was scheduled to be induced, but Mili had her own plans that day. When we were inspecting the house build prior to going to the hospital, she went into labour. She didn't tell me. I was oblivious that my little girl was on her way until we got to the hospital. Not long after being admitted, we found ourselves in the birthing suite. A few hours later, Mili entered the world on March 20, 2011. I will never forget the long, dark hair she was born with. She was perfect. My baby girl had arrived, and I was now the proud father of two princesses. I felt my world was perfect. What more could I want? This euphoria overrode the challenges that we had from a relationship perspective.

The next day, we introduced Bel, who was now three, to Mili. Her baby sister immediately besotted her. She just wanted to hold her and help feed her. It was cute to watch the two interact with each other. A few days after Mili's arrival, we headed for home. As with Bel, Ares had taken six months' leave. She would again get to spend a significant amount of time with Mili and Bel. Though this time I was not so jealous as I was getting the opportunity to take parental leave once, she returned to work. The three months that I had off and spent with both girls are some of the best months of my life. During this time, I laughed and cried; it was unforgettable. My love for these two had no bounds; it was deeper than the deepest ocean.

Over the 2011 October long weekend, we finally moved into the new house. By this stage, I hated the place. It didn't feel like the home I longed for. The house was very beige and neutral. Ares put a range of rules in place, which restricted how the house was lived in. These rules prevented things like the main bathroom from being used so it didn't get dirty, or the grout stained. This meant no soaking in the giant bathtub we had put in. It was all for show. The house felt cold, empty and lifeless.

Of an evening, I would come home from work, have something to eat and then go outside and work on the retaining walls, which surrounded the property. I would often work until 3 am before having a rest, then going to work. I had no choice; I wanted to spend as much time with my girls as I could, so I pushed myself hard. It became a bit of a challenge as neighbours would ask how much I planned on doing that night. Of all the nights I worked on those walls, the two nights when I disassembled the corner arc and rebuilt it were the most talked about. The night I rebuilt it; I worked through till the sun's rays illuminated the expansive horizon. The only reason I did this was to satisfy Ares, as she was not happy with the original radius. Doing things multiple times to appease her would become a pattern, which haunted me for years. Nothing was ever good enough for her. These instances only fuelled my dislike of the house. Her messaging of not being good enough is still firmly embedded in my psyche, a message I struggle to counteract to this day.

As the years passed, the relationship declined. I felt like a second-class citizen who was only in the house to serve her. One of the hardest things was watching how she treated Bel. Bel was no longer the centre of her world but relegated to second fiddle. It was clear to all that Mili was her favourite. I think this was probably because Mili is more like her mother than Bel. This crushed me, and I often had arguments about this favouritism. Her parents and her sister picked up on the relationship status and the impact it was having on me and the girls. At one stage, my then sister-in-law gave me child support forms and said that she and her husband would support me getting the girls out of the home. My mother-in-law also said to me she would not blame me when I left. Irrespective of these comments and what was going on, I stayed in the home. The thought of losing my girls kept me going.

At the time I didn't realise it, but I was living in a financially and emotionally abusive environment. For example, I would be regularly reminded that the only reason we had the house at Shell Cove was because of her, and my contributions were inadequate. When she started a tirade of abuse, everyone knew it. Neighbours would comment to me about the screaming that she did. Physically, she would also do various things to try to intimidate me, and I think hoped she would hurt me. I remember one occasion when she tried to physically attack me. She ran at me from across the room, but as she approached me, she slipped over, sliding into the lounge and breaking her foot. Another common occurrence was that she would slam doors in my face as I went to walk through them. I think she hoped that the door would hit me and hurt me. I didn't realise it, but what the girls and I were living in was a domestic violence situation.

Don't get me wrong; in amongst the bad times, we shared some amazing experiences together as a family. Every year, we would head to Umina and set up camp for four weeks. We had our site, which was near the amenities block, level and spacious. Each year, the setup got larger and more elaborate. It became our home away from home with a large undercover area between the camper and the walled gazebo, which was used as a dining area. The kids had a ball roaming the caravan park, swimming in the pools, and doing activities in the barn. I loved going along to the barn and helping them with their craft activities. As they got older, they loved going up to the BMX track outside the park and riding around. One year, I took Bel riding on some of the local mountain bike tracks. We had a ball. Watching them have so much fun gave me immense pleasure. I felt like I was giving the girls the opportunity to live their best lives. Over the years, we also made several trips to Queensland and the theme parks, along with a trip to Fiji.

A few years after moving into Shell Cove, Ares, and the girls asked me to do Christmas lights on the house. As with most things I do, I rarely do things by halves. This first year, I built a 7 m high light tree in the front yard and added some smaller decorations around the home. Little did I know, I had opened a Pandora's box. Each year, the Christmas lights multiplied exponentially. The house was now covered in lights. Over the years, we repeatedly won the best lights in Shell Cove. While winning was nice, the highlight for me was seeing all the fortunate people come and view the display. On the weekend, we would absorb the atmosphere sitting out the front of the house chatting with passersby and handing out lollipops to the children. I was truly happy. Seeing the smiles made me smile.

Over time, the relationship lows far outweighed the highs. We were spiralling, and it was becoming increasingly toxic in the home. I really knew that things were bad when Bel said to me one evening that she didn't understand why I stayed. This was a crushing blow as my then 13-year-old daughter had worked out how bad things had gotten. I started to question and evaluate why I was staying. I stayed in the relationship as I thought it was the best thing for the girls. Looking back, I know how wrong I was. All I was doing was showing them how a dysfunctional relationship looked. I was setting them up for failure in their future relationships.

Chapter 5

The Trip that Redefined my Life

---∞---

In 2019, I had planned a trip through Central Australia. I wanted to share my happy places with my family. With the date approaching, the COVID 19 pandemic kicked in. Borders were locked down, and I watched all my plans go out the window. I was devastated and worried about all the money I had laid out pre-booking things. An intense month followed as I negotiated refunds and, where I couldn't negotiate a refund, the fees would be treated as credit for a future date. In some ways, the pandemic was a blessing given I was not really prepared for the trip. I still had so much to do to get the ute, the camper, and the family ready for this epic adventure.

While the world shut down, I beavered away in the background. Upgrading the ute's suspension, the auxiliary power supply, storage system, and spares. The list was long, but I adopted the philosophy of how to eat an elephant. I took a bite at a time and over a few months progressively got things ready. The camper had its 12-volt system upgraded with the addition of a permanent solar panel and plug-in point for a solar blanket. I went over the ute and the trailer from tip to toe. I needed them to be as bulletproof as possible, as I was planning on dragging them across some unforgiving terrain.

By late 2020, glimmers of hope. Maybe we have this pandemic beat, or at least under control. Anticipating the borders would open, I started rebooking things for June and July 2021. I was still rolling the dice, but a roll I felt would come up trumps. The trip was locked in; the vehicles prepared and the family as prepared as they could be. It was going to be a bit of a trip into the unknown for them. I needed them to place trust in my planning and preparations as I knew what we were in for.

As the weeks passed, the departure date crept closer. I felt like all I was doing was getting ready for this trip. But I was deeply troubled, and work was not going well. The culture was terrible, and I felt like I was being crushed under its weight. The black dog set in and bit hard. One evening, I was called into the manager's office and questioned about some of my behaviours. I had no clue what they were talking about. Apparently, I was sitting at my desk stabbing myself in the head with a knife and balancing my chin on the tip. I had to trust that what I was being told was true. The work environment deeply troubled me, so it was plausible that I had completely disassociated. This trip away from work couldn't have come soon enough.

Day one arrived, and it was a simple but long highway drive. I wanted to get away relatively early so that we would not be arriving late that night. Unfortunately, Ares had other ideas and spent a large amount of time fluffing around the house. After we finally departed, she declared we needed to visit her grandparents and parents... We didn't get away until well after 10 am. At that point, I had already accepted that my idea of getting in at a reasonable hour was not a reality. This was further impacted by a leaking valve in one tyre, which required changing. Dinner that night was a bachelor's handbag — a roast chicken for those who don't know — bread rolls and salad from Coles, eaten next to a COVID testing tent in a truck stop. We still had hours to go before I could set up and get some rest, something that I eventually achieved at midnight. What a long day, and the trip had just begun. Was this to become the norm? I hoped not.

The next few days were spent travelling to and enjoying Lake Mungo. On the way in, we spent a few hours wandering the historic Yanga Homestead, built in 1870. The site comprises several buildings, including the original home and gardens on the edge of Yanga Lake. Not long after leaving the homestead, we hit the dirt for the first time. The road to Lake Mungo was in great condition, enabling us to make good time and arrive at our destination in daylight. The last time I visited was on a Uni field trip 20 years ago. On that trip, we had a catastrophic failure of one trailer, which we ended up leaving behind. Fortunately, the same fate was avoided this time around.

The rising sun filled the sky with colours of pink and purples prior to transitioning to spectacular reds and oranges. The sun's rays lit up the surrounding plains and highlighted the beauty of the historic woolshed and fenced yards. The sounds of native birds complemented the sunrise, welcoming in the morning and several kangaroos lapping up water from a low in the gravel carpark. Later that day, we joined the elder, who shared the Indigenous history of the lakes. I loved this as it complemented my geological knowledge of the landscape's evolution. The Great Wall section of the lake's lunette is a barren yet spectacular area characterised by shapely geological formations courtesy of thousands of years of wind and water erosion. The landscape is a photographer's dream with the light bouncing off the sedimentary structures. Spending a few days at the lake was a great way to kick off the trip.

After visiting Mungo, we kept heading north towards Broken Hill, an area steeped in mining history. What a surprise! We arrived late in the evening only to discover someone else occupied our allocated site. After finding a new site, we settled in for the night as the next few days were going to be busy sightseeing. The following morning, we headed underground and checked out a historic silver mine. A trip followed this to Silvertown, where we visited attractions such as the Mad Max Museum, and hunted for the famous donkeys that roam the town. Following a fruitless search, no donkeys were found, but we found piles of dung, so we knew they were there somewhere. The evening was spent overlooking Broken Hill from the sculpture park. With the sun setting, the sculptures lit up in all their glory, and I happily took photos trying to capture those memories in time. There was a genuine feeling of peace and serenity as the dark descended, and the cool night air enveloped us.

One full day left and so much to see… We can do it! Out with the maps, and we plotted our route. From one attraction to the next and then on again. We visited everything from historical ruins to art galleries. The highlight of the day was our visit to Bells Milk Bar, which had been operating since 1892. This place served the best milkshakes and waffles. The girls were in heaven, as was I. What a massive day that was. I was so glad to head for bed, as the following few days would have us travelling further north to Cameron Corner and then onto Innamincka.

History repeated. I was all packed up and ready to hit the road when Ares declared we needed to go to the shops. We were there yesterday… While we didn't have a long drive ahead; I had planned to stop at several historic sites along the way. After a few hours on the road, we reached Milparinka, where we turned off the bitumen and onto the dirt headed for Poole's Grave and Sturt's Cairn. The track conditions enabled us to make great time and reach the site of Poole's grave quickly. After a quick stop at the gravesite, we moved on to Sturt's Cairn, which sat atop Mt Poole. Mt Poole rose spectacularly from the surrounding plains as it reached for the blue sky. It was at this point I realised that the trek up to the cairn would not be easy, and I should expect some vocal complaints. Setting off, the track climbed steeply up the side of the mountain. The track was poorly defined and strewn with weather-beaten rocks. Climbing higher and higher, my thoughts turned to the serenity of the place, but also how formidable it must have been for Sturt and his team all those years ago. At the summit, Sturt's Cairn loomed large and afforded expansive views of the surrounding plains far below us. The Cairn is a formidable pile of rocks constructed purely to keep Sturt's team busy while they were encamped. I was glad that I was still over 100kg as the flies were threatening to carry me off while I absorbed the views. While this was a special experience, the highlight came on the descent. In the distance, my two girls were hand in hand, helping each other navigate the rocky path to the base of the mountain. This image of the two girls makes my heart sing to this day.

Back on the road, we continued heading for Cameron Corner. We still had several 100kms to cover, and the daylight hours were ticking away. I had resigned myself that this was going to be another late night. Reaching Tibooburra, we visited Sturt's memorial site, which includes an upturned whaling boat. It was amusing to see this boat, but back in the day, they thought there must have been an inland sea. The ute was refuelled, and we hit the last leg of our journey for the day. With darkness descending, we traversed the jump-ups heading for the border. By the time we reached the dog fence, it was pitch black and quite eerie. Through the fence, we could see the lights of the Corner Store twinkling in the distance. Our destination was in sight. After quickly setting up, we headed to the pub for what was best be described as a meal one wished they could forget.

The following morning, a spectacular sunrise welcomed in the day, as did the corner store's fuel tank. Painted on one end of the tank was the message, *"G'day and welcome to Cameron Corner. It's not the middle of nowhere; it's the centre of everywhere."* Cameron Corner felt like the centre of everywhere. After packing up, we stopped in at the border post where New South Wales, Queensland, and South Australia meet. The girls had fun while they danced around the post, transitioning from state to state and calling out the state they were in. It was a great way to start the day.

Chapter 5

Heading off towards Innamincka, the terrain changed. The rocky jump-ups gave way to the rolling dunes of the Strzelecki Desert. We arrived at Innamincka early afternoon and dropped the camper off before hitting the road again to visit some of the Burke and Wills historic sites. That afternoon, we crossed in and out of South Australia and changed time zones. We visited the Dig Tree, Burke and Wills' graves and the site where King was rescued. At the conclusion of another long but cup-filling day, we had dinner at the pub and chatted with one lady who worked there. Little did we know that a month later, we would meet her again in a different pub. That night I crashed early as tomorrow was going to be a long day and the first challenging day of driving, heading to Cordillo Downs and another corner post.

Waking that morning, I anxiously checked to see if the Cordillo Downs road had been opened following the rains and flooding. We caught a break, and it was opened that morning. Not long after setting off, we had to navigate a muddy creek and a series of very boggy sections. By this point, 4WD was engaged, and forward momentum slowed. Pushing further along the track, we continued to encounter bog holes, which had us sliding sideways and the girls squealing with excitement. As the sand dunes gave way to more open plains, we started seeing feral camels, emus, and dingos, frequently stopping to take photos. In the distance, we started getting our first glimpses of what we saw. The historic Cordillo Downs woolshed. The shed was bigger than I had expected it to be. It was an impressive structure constructed of rock and corrugated iron. Following lunch and some repairs to the stone stopper, which had filled with mud, we backtracked and headed for the lesser-known corner post, Hadden's Corner. The Gibber Plains extended as far as the eye could see. It's hard to comprehend that people called this area home and made a living out here. Eventually, the Gibber Plains were consumed by an increasing number of small sand dunes as we approached the turnoff to get to the corner. At the turnoff, I had a decision to make: Do I drop the camper or drag it through the dunes? By this stage, the day was getting on, and I pushed on with the camper in tow. As we weaved our way through the dunes, I was pleasantly surprised at how well the ute and camper performed. Like Cameron Corner, the girls danced their way around the post, which marked the northeastern point where Queensland and South Australia meet. What was even better was that this was where I had planned to spend the night, and I still had hours of daylight left. But my excitement was quickly trodden on with a declaration of, *"I don't feel safe; we are not staying here.!"*

Following Ares's declaration, we headed for Birdsville, several hours away. Fortunately, we could make good time as the development track was in great condition. Along the way into Birdsville, we stopped at the Rainbow Serpent art installation created from local stone and gibbers. The serpent is symbolic to the local indigenous people and represents the waterways, which dissect the channel country. With night falling, I was still over 100km away from our destination. I knew it was going to be another late one. Pulling into the caravan park, we found a spot and set up camp for the night. We would deal with the extra night's camping in the morning.

The sun's rays broke the black of the night, and the corella choir sang. The air was filled with the sounds of a new day. The spectacular colours that flooded the sky enhanced these sounds. The initial dark purples and pinks gave way to intense yellows and oranges. What a magical start to the day! We were to witness several more spectacular sunrises over the coming days. Our first full day in Birdsville was spent moving to our site, then carrying out repairs on the camper, followed by some fun on Big Red. Big Red is a famous dune that marks the start/end of the Simpson Desert crossing. After letting the tyres down, we crested the dune and parked. To the west of us, we could make out the track that we were to drive the following day. The track stretched out across the desert and disappeared over the crest of the second dune we would cross. While on top of the dune, we did some sand boarding, racing down the dune against each other. After each eating enough sand to make a sandcastle while sand boarding, we headed back to camp for an early night, as tomorrow was going to be a long day.

By 7 am, we had stopped off at the Birdsville bakery, stocking up on pies and sausage rolls. I even tried one of the camel pies, and I must say I was impressed. Once supplies for the day were sorted, we drove 50km west back to Big Red to start our trip to Poppel Corner, which designates the junction between Queensland, South Australia, and the Northern Territory. While we only had a little over 150 km to do each way, this was going to be an all-day challenge. As we crested dune after dune, we inched closer to our goal. The desert is a magical place; it's not desolate but full of life. Low woody shrubs characterised the dunes and the plains, and vibrant wildflowers flourished because of the recent rains. As we were heading west, we tackled the steep sides of all the dunes. This tested both me as the driver and the ute. But thankfully, both were up to the task, and we made it to the Corner at about 1 pm without getting bogged once. We spent a little over an hour at the Corner before starting the trek back to the east.

I was expecting the return leg to be an easier run as we would tackle the dunes from the less steep side. I was wrong. The western side of the dunes was badly cut up and rutted, making going slow. Dinner was spent trackside and shared with the flies. As the hours ticked past, I knew we would end up driving into the night, something I was not looking forward to. At night, the desert has a beautiful eeriness about it. It is still, calm and very dark. With all the ute's lights breaking the darkness, we pushed on, eventually making it back to Big Red. But we wanted to be at Little Red, a smaller section of the dune, which would be easier to drive at night. But alas, I could not find the track.

The ute's radio crackled to life as a group on top of the dune encouraged me to take on Big Red's hardest track. It was 8:30 at night; I was tired and hadn't driven the track in daylight, let alone in the dark. I lined the ute up and went for it. I thought we were going to make it, but no, we sank into the soft sand at the very crest of the dune. Our escape had been stopped a few metres short. The guys at the top of the dune cheered us on as I backed down the dune, which was very challenging in the night's darkness. On my second attempt, we crested the dune. Our epic day trip to the Corner was almost at an end. All that was left was the easy 50 km sealed road back to the caravan park.

The following day was a rest day. Well, this is a rest day by my standards. Once we crawled out of bed, we returned to the dune and played on the various tracks up and down its face. It was so much easier and less daunting in the light of day. That afternoon, the fuel tank was filled, and we settled in for an early night as the next day would have us cover over 700 km to Longreach.

Longreach is a major town in Central Queensland, where we planned on spending a few days to take in the sights and relax. We arrived in town as the sun was setting, and the rain was falling. Setting up was not fun after that drive. But tomorrow was always another day. There were many highlights during our time in Longreach. They included a ride on a stagecoach through the town. Both girls rode up front next to the driver, which made it even more special for them. We visited the Qantas Museum, and that night watched the spectacular show they project onto the body of the museum's planes. One of the other highlights of our time was a visit to the School of the Air. This made the girls realise how good they had it going to an actual school.

After a few days, we made our way to Winton, home of the dinosaurs. As a geologist, I was really looking forward to this part of the trip. After setting up camp, we backtracked and visited the Age of Dinosaurs Museum. While there, we checked out the fossil processing area, where teams extracted bones from the surrounding sediments. I was really getting my nerd on. The following day, we hit the dirt and headed for Lark Quarry. Walking around the in situ fossilised footprints took me back to a time long ago. In front of us lay exposed one of the largest trackways known to exist. The preserved footprints dart to the left and the right, with some crossing the footprints of the larger animals. We were all in awe of what stretched out before us. As the sun set on another day, we returned to town for the evening. This was to be our last in Queensland.

We left Winton and headed west towards the Northern Territory border, along the Plenty Highway. The road was straight and narrow as it tracked its way across the barren landscape. In the distance, a cloud of dust was visible and looked to be moving in our direction. It turned out to be a helicopter mustering cattle. It was amazing to watch the pilot skilfully dart and dive around just metres off the ground. The sealed road gave way to dirt, so we knew we were remote and had the road to ourselves. We made great time because of the road conditions and lack of other vehicles. Late that afternoon, we crossed into the Northern Territory, stopping to take photos of the border sign. Further along the track, we came to a screeching halt as a termite mound filled the windscreen. This thing was the size of a bus; I couldn't believe termites built it.

Setting off early the next morning, we kept tracking west headed for Alice Springs. The road conditions were relatively good, which allowed us to travel safely at close to 100kmh. About two hours up the road, I was caught out hitting a patch of bull dust covering an extremely corrugated section. The van was thrown sideways, with the side filling my rearview mirror. Not only could I see the side of the van, but I could see the pole bag trying to exit the carrier. The trip had taken its toll, and the pole bag had broken a hole in the carrier. Glad I spotted that one. After a roadside repair, we continued, arriving at our planned overnight stop, Gemtree, at lunchtime. On inspection, we were not overly enthused about staying there, so we pushed on to Alice Springs. It felt great to pull into Alice early. It meant an extra day of rest as this marked the halfway point in our trip.

They say that life is not meant to be easy, and I discovered that at the caravan park. We had been allocated a shady site for the week, but its configuration meant we could not set the camper up. After much back and forth with the park management, we were allocated a new site. This one was even better, given it was larger and on a corner, making access easy. Once set up, it was time to relax as tomorrow was, in essence, a free day. A day where I could buy what I needed and undertake maintenance and repairs to the camper and the ute.

The following day, we set off into Alice to buy the parts I needed and get some groceries. While this seemed mundane, it turned into one of the most interesting experiences of the trip. The government declared an emergency three-day lockdown. The town went nuts, so we headed to Coles to get our groceries, with our supplies running low. Ares and my youngest went into the shop while my eldest and I waited in the ute. They thought that it was going to be a straightforward exercise. No, it was crazy in there. They even had police patrolling the shop. At one stage, a police officer approached my youngest and asked her if she was lost. Her mum had sent her off to find lollies for her and her sister. I got a call and headed into the shop, not knowing what I was walking into. It was complete madness. But we survived that experience, got fuel and had a decision to make. Do we go back to the site, or do we escape the lockdown and head out of town to check out one site we wanted to visit? Us being us; we took the latter and made a beeline for Palm Valley.

Tyres deflated, we started crawling our way into the valley. While not a technical drive, there were a few moments where I had to stop and pick lines crossing creeks and rock shelves. As we got closer to the valley, the cliff walls closed in, and the vegetation transitioned from scraggly, stunted desert shrubs and eucalypts to denser and lusher vegetation. We had reached the valley, and it didn't disappoint. At the end of the road, we parked and headed off on foot deeper into the valley. The deeper we went, the more spectacular it became. This was truly a special place. Heading back into town, with the sun slowly setting, the stillness of the night became clear. We were in good spirits; we had snuck in some sightseeing before returning to lockdown. On the way back to camp, we were half expecting to be stopped by the police, but we didn't see any.

The following day was spent doing washing and maintenance tasks. It was great to be forced to stop for a few days; I needed the rest; we all needed the rest. That morning, there was a constant stream of vans leaving the park and heading out of town. About two hours later, all the vans returned. The police had blocked the road and were not letting anyone leave town. I found this quite amusing, given what we had done the day before. Both girls spent much of the day entertaining themselves in the play area, but I was pleasantly surprised when they helped and cleaned the inside of the car for me. As with all things COVID, the rumours circulated that the lockdown might be lifted a day earlier than originally shown. With this news, we packed the car so that if it lifted early, we could go exploring straight away. That evening, we kicked back and enjoyed the sunset along with a cold beverage…

By mid-morning the following day, it was announced that lockdown would be lifted at 12. Now to make plans, what to do that afternoon. After much deliberation, all of 30 seconds, we headed west for the afternoon to see what we could find along the way. We ended up at a lookout and could see

Gosses Bluff in the distance. We had come this far, so why not go further and check the place out? As we wound our way along the corrugated track, the scale of the site became clear. Cliffs rising steeply from the plains surrounded us. It is hard to describe the enormity of the impact site; it was all-encompassing.

As always, the following days were full-on. We didn't stop. One day, we explored the East Macdonald Ranges. The next day, the West Macdonald Ranges and their spectacular gorges. Over the following few days, we visited just about every tourist attraction in Alice. Stops included the Reptile Centre, the Telegraph Station, the Botanic Garden, ANZAC Hill, the Alice Springs Brewery, and the Desert Park. Of all these sites, my highlight was the Desert Park nocturnal tour. If you are ever fortunate enough to get to Alice, the nocturnal tour is a must-do.

We left Alice and headed for Uluru, but I was hit with a wave of fatigue. I had been driving continuously for several weeks, along with setting up and packing down camp. It was at this point that I had to ask Ares to drive for a while. It felt great not to be driving, but I don't think she was happy with the role reversal. After a few hours, we swapped seats again. Lunch was spent at the Erldunda service station, a few hundred km from Uluru. While we were there, the girls fed the emus, which were kept on site. It was hilarious watching them tentatively put their hands out to be then pecked at by a giant bird. Once back on the road, we were overtaken by a ute pulling a van at speed. It was crazy how fast the driver was going. Not long after, we came across the same van on the side of the road with two blown tyres. They were lucky they didn't flip when the tyres let go.

We arrived at our campground relatively early; we set up and headed to Uluru. Approaching Uluru, its scale consumed us. I will admit that, even though I had seen it before, it still made me stop and reflect on its majestic beauty. My inner geologist kicked in, and I started taking in the bedding plains and other geological features. That night, we got to see the rock in a peculiar light. We went to the Field of Lights and watched the sunset over the rock from a nearby dune with drinks and canapes. Once the sunset, the Field of Lights came to life. The coloured carpet spreading over the desert was truly spectacular.

The following day was a long and hard day as we walked the 10 km track that circumnavigated the rock. While it was flat, it was challenging not only because of the heat but more so because of the density of flies. They were thick, and I am positive, a few ended up being protein snacks for us… Despite the challenges, the walk gives you a true sense of the rock's scale and beauty. Later that afternoon, we headed out to Kata Tjuta and took the short Walpa Gorge walk surrounded by the towering conglomerate domes. We could not stay for very long as later that evening; we were taking a camel ride to watch another spectacular sunset over the rock.

Beep, beep, beep. The alarm clock was ringing loud and clear, yet it was still pitch-black outside. Today was a day I had been looking forward to. We were heading back out towards Kata Tjuta to watch the sunrise over the rock. While we took our positions, the first rays of light pierced the black sky and turned it a magnificent purple colour. As the sun continued to rise, the purple gave way to the golden glow of what turned out to be another spectacular day exploring Kata Tjuta's domes on the Valley of the Winds trail. While the Ares and Mili stopped at the first lookout, Bel and I pushed on and headed for Karingana Lookout, which was the saddle between two of the domes. The view in either direction was breathtaking. Personally, I think Kata Tjuta is far more spectacular than Uluru, because of its construction and the eroded shape of the domes. That evening was spent watching the stars and planets on an astronomy tour.

The next day was a relaxed pack up as we only had a relatively short drive. We had lunch at the Mt Conner Station halfway to our destination. It felt good to be taking it easy for a change, especially knowing that the next few days were going to be hard dirt driving. Once refuelled and the ute's tank topped up, we were off again, thinking that in a few hours we would be set up, and I would enjoy a cold beer in the bar. Things didn't quite work out like that as the girls wanted to stop and feed the emus again. This time, they were a little less apprehensive and happily fed the emus. With less than 80 km of sealed road to our destination, we could take in the sights. That night, we set up at Kulger Pub and witnessed another mystical outback sunset. This was to be our last night in the Northern Territory.

Early the following day, we hit the dirt headed for Mt Dare. We were again fortunate that the road conditions were great, and we could make good time. Approaching Mt Dare, we spotted a trailer on the side of the road with many cameras mounted to it. We had no clue what it was until we got to Mt Dare Station, and they informed us it was number plate recognition to see if we were entering South Australia with a valid COVID travel permit. This was not an issue as we had a permit. Later that afternoon, we headed to Dalhousie Springs. Lush green vegetation juxtaposed with the barren desert surrounding the Springs. As I floated around in the warm water, it felt like all my cares had been washed away. I was so relaxed. The drive back to Mt Dare was made all the better by a stunning sunset. The sky came to life with a range of yellows and oranges. What a way to end the day!

Chapter 5

On returning to Mt Dare Station, Ares was a little taken aback after heading to the bathroom. When she entered, she read a sign warning of dingo activity in the area. This sign had her on high alert. I'm not convinced she slept much that night. She was also very cautious in the morning heading for the shower. But we all lived to tell the story. In reality, there was a greater chance of flies carrying us off than of a dingo.

The sky was grey and ominous looking as we set off towards William Creek. Floods had damaged the direct route, so we had to take the detour roads, which added an extra 200 km to the day. It was already going to be a long day on the road without the detour. Back tracking northwest towards Fink, the rain started falling. At first, it was only light showers, but it was enough to make the track slippery. With 4WD high engaged, we pushed on, finally turning south onto Hamilton Station Road. The rain eventually gave way to sunshine, which appeared to dry the track out. Just past the station, the track conditions were appalling at best. The mud was thick, and there was no other option but to hit it at speed or be trapped by the sludge that it was. Driving at speed in those circumstances comes with risk, especially when towing. Numerous times, the ute and the camper were at 90 degrees to each other as we slid our way down the road towards Oodnadatta. I think the most amusing part of the trip was when we were stopped by a guy driving a Porsche heading in the opposite direction. We gave him a heads-up about the track and wished him luck. He was planning to drive across the Simpson Desert to raise funds for motor neurone disease.

Following lunch at the Pink Roadhouse, we continued towards William Creek, checking out sights such as Algebuckina Bridge. William Creek is a speck on the map in the middle of nowhere, with not much more than a pub, fuel station, and airport to it. Though if you are a stargazer, the place is phenomenal as there is no light pollution. That night, I sat for hours, watching the stars of the Milky Way, shooting stars and satellites tracking across the night sky. The lack of light pollution means you can even see what look like gas clouds filling the void between the stars. I was so inspired by what I could see; I had a go at some astrophotography with mixed results. While I stared into the sky that night, little did I know that my world would soon change trajectory.

Rusty Rails

The rails of the old Ghan line lay stretched out before me

They guide my vision towards the Algebuckina Bridge

A rusted iron behemoth from a time long past

The two rails merge into one

Lost in a shimmering mirage created by the heat of the desert

How many people have crossed this bridge?

Where were their journeys taking them?

What were they hoping to find at the end of the line?

In such a hostile part of the world

Click, click, click

The camera shutter snaps shut

A moment in time immortalised in black and white

But the image screams of colour

The unspoken power of the rusty rails and that bridge is yet to be discovered

The rusty rails stretching across the bridge align my mind
Guiding me on my way
Just as they guided the trains all those years ago
The rails draw me in deeper and deeper
The thoughts become clear

My life will never be the same as it was that day
The day I set foot on that bridge and stared into the distance
The day I wondered whose journeys had crossed this point
The day I realised I needed to rethink my journey through life

While my journey of discovery has just begun
It is a journey of growth
A metamorphosis
A transition
It is a journey of hope
A journey guided by the image of the rusty rails
And the iron behemoth Algebuckina Bridge stretching into the distance
I am not who I once thought I was
I am not who others think I am
I am not who others want me to be
Instead
I am who I am, and I am me

Chapter 5

The following morning, we set off bright and early as we had a long drive and lots to see along the way. Making our way south, we came upon the Kati Thanda (Lake Eyre) turnoff. To this day, I can't explain why I turned left and drove to the lake as it was not part of my itinerary. The road was long and rocky as we traversed the desolate Gibber Plains, before descending onto the lake foreshore and driving at elevations below sea level. Kati Thanda is a surreal place to visit. It had been 20 years since I had last been there.

Once you cross the lunettes that surround the lake, your eyes are drawn towards the horizon, where the blue sky kisses the glistening white salt crust. Along the shore of the lake are several small rocky outcrops that the wind, salt, and water have shaped over thousands of years. I remember walking over to the outcrop to check it out and take some photos of my girls, photos that I will cherish for a lifetime. I tentatively walked out onto the lake's surface and started walking towards the horizon. I was half expecting to sink up to my knees in the mud like I had the last time I walked on the lake's surface. I did not know how far I was going to get, or what I was going to do when I got there. I instantly felt at one with the lake and the environment, which was surrounding me. I was also comforted knowing that I was sharing this place with my two daughters.

I continued to walk further from the shoreline; I felt a feeling I had never felt before. It was a euphoric feeling. It was at this time that I admitted to myself that I had spent my life hiding behind a façade. A façade I had constructed over many years. But I did not yet know exactly what the façade was hiding. Standing there, I felt like a great weight had been lifted off my shoulders. The lifting of this weight may explain why I could walk so far out without sinking in the mud...

As I walked back across the lake, my brain was racing. Taking that left-hand turn was the catalyst for one of the most significant turning points in my life. A lot was to unfold over the coming months.

After an hour, we made our way back to the ute, backtracking to where we turned off before resuming our trip south towards the Flinders Ranges. Along the way, we stopped at the Mutonia Sculpture Park on the Oodnadatta Track. The park comprises an eclectic mix of sculptures made from scrap. The most notable sculpture comprises the fuselages of two planes standing on their tails. Other stops included Marree and Farina, prior to making it to Blinman late that evening. We were so late that we only caught the kitchen as it was closing for the evening. I don't think they were that impressed, receiving our dinner order five minutes before close.

Chapter 5

The night was a wild one with gale-force winds and heavy rain. The canvas of the van flapped and bashed in the wind like a loose sail. The winds were so strong they were making the van rock. The sound of the wind was deafening, offset only by the loud thunderclaps. Lightning effortlessly danced across the night sky, momentarily breaking the darkness. Eventually, tiredness won, and I drifted off to sleep, only to be woken by the sound of canvas tearing. The wind had caught and lifted the solar blanket attached to the roof and tore the mounting points. This same gust also bent the camper's frame, issues that I would deal with once we got back from the trip.

Despite the rain, I was really looking forward to the day. We were going to be driving through one of Australia's geological masterpieces, Brachina Gorge. Yep, I got my rock nerd on as we drove the 20 km of track and traversed 130 million years of Earth's history. I have been to the Gorge several times but had never been to the golden spike, a significant geological marker. While the rain fell and the cold wind cut through me, I left the other three huddled in the ute warm and dry. I was determined to find the spike and check the site out. After about an hour, I returned to the ute, resembling a drowned rat but smiling ear to ear. I had done it and ticked that goal off. Exiting the Gorge, we turned south. I thought we had just driven the last of the dirt for the trip. The rest would be back on sealed roads, and mostly in civilisation, as we started making our way home. Late that evening, we pulled into Gawler and set up for the night.

The following day was a relaxed day as we drove the few hours to the coastal town of Victor Harbour. Along the way, I followed some of the Tour Down Under cycling route and was amazed at how steep some sections in the Adelaide foothills were. We checked out the big rocking horse and had lunch at a Germanic pub in Hahndorf. We wandered the streets of Hahndorf for a while before continuing on our way to Victor Harbour, arriving mid-afternoon. I had forgotten how to set the camper up in daylight; it was just something that rarely happened. Even better, I had planned this to be a rest stop.

Over the few days we were there, the COVID situation ramped up, and Victoria closed its borders. This threw a spanner in the works, as we had planned to head home via Victoria. Quickly assessing our options, we headed across to Kangaroo Island for a few days, booking the ferry the following day. In the interim, we continued to explore the area, blissfully unaware of the next challenge we would face. Driving along the beach returning from the Murray River's mouth, the radio crackled to life, announcing a soft lockdown, which restricted the opening of several of the tourist attractions we were planning on visiting on Kangaroo

Island. With this news, we tried to cancel our ferry ticket, but we were told we would lose the fare if we did, given they were an essential service and excluded from the lockdown rules. We had no choice but to head to Kangaroo Island the following day.

Heading west, the radio discussion suggested that the soft lockdown may be ramped up to a hard lockdown of the South Australia border. If the State went into lockdown, and we were still there, we didn't know how long we would be stuck. We arrived at the port and again tried to get our money back for the ferry, but we were denied. The next few hours were spent waiting for the 1 pm announcement regarding the lockdown. As suggested, the Premier confirmed the state would be locked down from 6 pm, and no one could enter or leave the state. With alarm bells ringing in my head, Ares went back into the terminal and demanded our money be refunded. While she was doing this, I was hatching the escape plan.

All roads lead back to Broken Hill, but we couldn't go into Victoria to get there, and we wouldn't make the border following the highway; it was just too far. My only option was to head for Renmark and then take several dirt tracks to pick up the Silver City Highway in New South Wales. Leaving Renmark, we started on the first of the dirt tracks and came across what appeared to be a roadwork site with detour signs in place. But what we had come across was a police checkpoint set up to prevent people entering and exiting the state via the back roads I had planned to take. Luckily, we were waved through and kept heading for the border. I was so stressed about whether we would make it out by 6 pm that I crossed an unassuming cattle grid and realised that I was back in NSW. It was 5:50 pm. We had just made it, and I was exhausted, but knew I still had several hours to go before reaching Broken Hill again.

After a chaotic day, it was decided that the following day would be spent regrouping and working out our new plans going forward. After much discussion, it was decided that we would head from Broken Hill to Lightning Ridge, a drive of close to 800km. Lightning Ridge held a special place in Ares's heart as she had spent time there as a child on her grandfather's mining claim. As we were exploring again, we took the back roads from Wilcannia to Bourke. This drive was well worth it; we regularly spotted emus and kangaroos on the side of the road. The only downside was that this route took a lot longer than expected. It was late afternoon by the time we got to Burke, some 350 km short of our final destination. I knew I was going to be in for another late night behind the wheel and an even later night setting up for the next few days.

Chapter 5

Lightning Ridge is an interesting place to visit. It's like a vegetated moonscape with mineshafts dotted all around the town. One of the old mines has been turned into an underground sculpture installation called Chamber of the Black Hand. As you walk the old tunnels, various carvings ranging from large biblical figures to smaller carvings of famous people can be viewed. Other highlights of our time in Lightning Ridge included the hot baths, pubs in the scrub and the car door tours. One tour took us to a lookout on the western edge of town. The sunsets from this vantage point were to die for.

After a few days relaxing, by our standards, we headed off on the second-last leg of our trip. Our goal was to get to Dubbo so we could check out the zoo and see if we could leave the girls at the jail. Unfortunately, when we got to the jail, they determined the girls were too much, and we had them for life. Despondent with that revelation, we spent two days exploring the zoo together. I will admit I'm not a fan of zoos, but Western Plains is good, based on its open free-range design. Other than the jail and the zoo, Dubbo has very little going for it, so we moved on to Bathurst.

There are several ways to get to Bathurst from Dubbo, but as usual, we took the long way. I wanted to take the girls to Parkes to see The Dish, the radio telescope made famous by its role in the first and subsequent lunar landings. We spent a couple of hours at the site before hitting the road again, aiming for Forbes and then Eugowra, where my mother's family are from. We called in at the family farm to stretch the legs and say hi, prior to making our way to Bathurst and what was to be our last few nights on the road. Approaching Bathurst, we got a message saying that our accommodation booking had been cancelled because of COVID restrictions placed on the Greater Sydney area. Panicked, we contacted the caravan park and explained where we had been and that we were not coming from home, which had been a part of the locked-down area. Our explanation was not good enough for the lady we spoke to; she wanted to see proof. Thankfully, we had been keeping all the booking slips for the trip, so we could prove where we had been once, we got to the caravan park. By this stage, I was exhausted, having clocked up close to 10,000 km in the eight weeks we were away. That night, I slept well, knowing that tomorrow was going to be a relaxed day, as I would not be driving long distances.

Well, so much for that plan! The next morning, we were up relatively early, planning the day's adventures. The first thing that we did was do a few laps of the Mt Panorama racing circuit. The ute handled like a dream at 60 km/h. Not convinced it would be any good much faster than that… Once the novelty of lapping the mountain wore off, we headed to Orange and surrounds to visit the wineries. Where was my rest? I was back behind the wheel, driving kilometres on what I wanted as a day off, given the next day was the day that we drove home. Maybe I could rest then.

Although we were having a good time, I kept reflecting on my revelation from Kati Thanda. What did it mean? I guess time would tell…

Chapter 6

Six Months of Hell

---∞---

We woke the following morning to a pea-thick fog blanketing the caravan park. It was so thick it was difficult to see the full length of the van when standing in front of it. What made this fog special was the very fine snow that was falling. This magical white powder coating the camper and the ute was juxtaposed with the red dust from where we had been. If it hadn't been for the snow falling, the fog was very reminiscent of our first morning at Darlington Point all those weeks ago. Packing up in the snow was a challenge, as everything I touched was icy cold and slippery. Persistence paid off, and we headed out of town for home. We were on the last leg.

Arriving home, we were greeted by the family dog, Maya, a beautiful Husky that we had adopted a few years prior. She was so excited she just spun around in circles, not knowing who to greet first. My moment of relaxation was short-lived as the unpacking began almost immediately. I really didn't feel up to it but was really given no choice, so I begrudgingly set the camper up and started emptying it of its contents. With a mountainous pile of washing to do, the washing

Chapter 6

machine ran for days on end. By this time, I had come down from the high of the trip and realised that I really needed to unpack what was hiding behind the façade. Who was I? What was I about? And was I really hiding behind a facade? Questions I had but answers I was yet to discover.

As was the case prior to the trip, Ares and I slept in separate areas of the house. She moved into the spare bedroom, and I returned to sleeping in the master bedroom, a space I would become very familiar with over the coming months. Little did I know that this room would become my protective bubble as I unpacked my world, peeling back the layers of the onion, and exposing my soft underbelly. Over the next six months, I had a series of revelations. I had begun my journey of discovery; it was my six months of emotional hell as the façade crumbled around my feet. The ultimate mid-life crisis, one could say.

The first genuine revelation related to my marriage. We had been married for close to 20 years — a long time. For years, people had been pointing out how toxic and abusive the marriage was. My in-laws had even said to me that when I leave, they wouldn't blame me. Now, saying something like that is huge and comes with so many alarm bells. Nevertheless, I ignored it and pushed on. I was determined to give the girls their best life but blinded by the fact I was destroying their lives by staying in such a hostile environment. However, now that I had questioned everything, I could see the situation for myself. I knew that the marriage was over.

Even though I had come to this conclusion, I kept it locked away inside. I felt guilt and shame over the fact that my marriage had failed. I continued isolating myself to protect myself and, I thought, protect Ares and the kids from how I felt. All I could see, and feel was pain and anguish for all concerned. I wished the world would open up and swallow me. The pain was immense. This was exactly the opposite of what I was hoping for in my life. When we were first together, I gave her a crystal rose and a mirror base with the inscription that said, 'Like this rose, my love for you will never die'. I gave her an identical one on our wedding day with an inscription saying, 'My love for her had blossomed'. I wanted to be happily married to my best friend. But the love we once shared abandoned me. I felt it had abandoned her as well.

In my confused state, I did not know what this looked like. That I was yet to work out. Would we stay together and live separate lives? Would we go our own ways? Or would I just dig another big hole and bury how I felt? I initially chose the latter, thinking it would be best for all, but it just ate at my soul, and I spiralled further into depression. It took another 10 months for the true manifestation of this revelation to become apparent. It was the 26th of June 2022 when Ares declared, during an argument, that it was over, and we needed to go our separate ways. This declaration rocked me to my core. It was the realisation of my worst fear.

The next question that arose while deconstructing the façade related to my sexuality. I felt confused; I was no longer attracted to Ares. This felt strange, given how promiscuous I was in my teens and early 20s. What had changed? Was I gay? Was I attracted to men? The answer to the gay question was simple. I had no desire to be with men. I was still attracted to females, just not sexually. A part of me breathed, but the situation confused me. I didn't have the language to describe how I was feeling. It was strange and foreign to me. It was much later that the language became clear.

I started opening up to close friends in the queer community about how I was feeling, hoping they could help me understand. These conversations exposed me to a whole new vocabulary. I was learning the words I needed. My anxiety about how I was feeling progressively lifted; my understanding blossomed. I was introduced to the concept of asexuality. Asexuality is used to describe someone who is not sexually attracted to individuals of any gender. I adopted this new language to describe my sexuality, yet it was not a perfect fit. Further exploration and soul-searching were needed.

Being a neurospicy research nerd, I dived the rabbit hole of asexuality. There had to be more to it. Well, that's what I thought. And I was right. The more conversations I had, and the more reading I did, the more I realised that asexuality was not a fixed sexual orientation but a spectrum. A spectrum that I now hoped would capture how I was feeling. Was I aceflux, aegosexual, apothisexual, cupiosexual, demisexual, grey or lithosexual? With all these identities, surely one would fit me. As I researched each one, it became clear I was demisexual. Specifically, for me to be sexually attracted to someone, I needed to have a strong emotional connection with them. Even when this connection is established, the sexual attraction I felt was rare. With this new understanding, I could explain why I was no longer sexually attracted to Ares and why, historically, I had a low desire to be intimate with her, despite loving her. Another piece of the puzzle fell into place, and more of the façade that I portrayed, came down. Brick by brick, it was crumbling.

By late 2021, my mental health was spiralling out of control. All the thoughts and feelings really overwhelmed me. I felt I had no one to turn to, so I kept pushing on, in silence and isolation. But in doing so, all I was achieving was reinforcing the positive feedback loop of depression. It was not uncommon for me to cry myself to sleep at night. I had stopped functioning, such as not eating or looking after my personal hygiene. I was falling apart but discovered the authentic me. While much of the façade remained, I still felt uncomfortable in my skin.

Despite the discomfort and the battle with depression, I had to keep peeling the layers of the onion. I had to keep trying to find out what was behind the façade. I needed to discover who I was and what the values were by which I wanted to live. I was an emotional mess, and everyone around me knew it. I distanced myself progressively further, particularly from my girls. I wanted to protect them from the turmoil. My self-absorption was doing more damage to my relationship with them than I thought.

By December 2021, I had worked out many parts of the puzzle I was hiding behind. I was not being true and authentic, but what was that? One thought kept coming up over this time, and it was that I always felt uncomfortable in my skin. But why was I so uncomfortable now? I needed to work out what was going on. For most of my life, I had always put that feeling down to the abuse I was exposed to as a child. This feeling ran deep. It penetrated my core. There had to be more to it. It was at this point that I started writing notes, trying to unpack my world. Many of those notes have evolved into the story that you are reading now. It was my first crack at trying to see past the last part of the façade.

Over several weeks, I recalled the times when I dressed as female as a younger child and into my teens and early adult life. I recalled that I had never felt like I was a boy. I felt like I was trapped in a shell that was not mine. Initially, I thought that I was a cross-dresser, but I didn't do it for pleasure, so I ruled that one out quickly. My only other alternative was that I was transgender. But no way...

For 44 years, I had not been overtly exposed to members of the transgender community. I was oblivious to the community's structure, needs, wants and just the scale of the community. To be honest, I was in the same boat for the broader rainbow community. While I had colleagues and friends who identified as being members of the community, I was disconnected from it. This lack of contact was isolating. Who can I turn to? Where can I go? I did not know. It was like going into a fight with both hands tied behind your back. Here I was, questioning my identity but with no one to bounce my feelings and thoughts off; it was hard. I still needed to work out whether these thoughts of being trans were real.

Not long after realising I might be transgender, I set up a new Facebook account under my preferred name, Carla. A name that had been with me all my life. If Carla could not live in the real world, then she could at least live in the virtual world that is social media. I had my privacy settings so high

Chapter 6

I couldn't even find myself from my alternative profile. This was to be private, invite-only, just as I wanted to handle Carla's emergence. It was to be by invitation only, as I still hadn't confirmed in my mind that Carla was real or a fleeting figment of my imagination.

One of the first things I did was cast a net out, as I tried to find any and every transgender-related group/page on the platform. I was trying to find answers to questions that, mostly; I hadn't even planned in my mind. I felt the exercise was akin to a fisherperson casting their nets and not knowing what they were going to catch. As I started reviewing my catch, my eyes were opened. Here was this diverse and eclectic mix of groups that I hadn't even contemplated would or should have existed. To be truthful, a lot of what I had discovered was confronting, somewhat disturbing and scary. But within the net were some nuggets of gold. These nuggets of gold would form the basis for building a sense of belonging within the trans community.

I had found a few Australian-based groups, which appeared to be about supporting people like me. I tentatively submitted join requests and was subsequently accepted. Was this my first step to finding my tribe, my people? I vividly recalled that my first post on these pages included a very brief introduction and highlighted my uncertainty regarding my gender identity. A face app edited image of myself accompanied the post. The post, like all social media posts, got a few comments, some useful and some just a waste of bits and bytes. One response came from a lady, Bec, who lived not that far from me. Over a period of a few weeks, we regularly exchanged messages. Ironically, we both went to the same all-boys Catholic school, just a few years apart. What good examples of ERC old boys we had become. A fact that still makes me laugh today. With time, this online friendship developed. She became my online rock within the community. These messages were my first real interaction with a member of the trans community, a community that I was yet to accept I was part of. It was during this time, and through the messages, that I solidified my identity. Yes, I am trans. I was trapped in the wrong body and had always been, hence why my skin suit never felt right.

Chapter 7

Belonging

---∞---

While online, I was building an international network; my face-to-face community was very limited. For example, it took several months for Bec and I to meet face to face, even though we lived minutes away. This lack of genuine connection impacted my sense of belonging to a community. It was like my community existed out there somewhere but was distant, even when close.

Why was this the case? I thought birds of a feather flock together. It felt quite the opposite, to be truthful. Reality was, I had lost sight of one of my first lessons in that, while we are all transgender, we don't appear to flock together. I think the innate desire to integrate, to blend into the cis community, underpins the distal element to be seen only as our true gender. But I will always be trans, as much as I wish it were not the case. I'm fortunate that I have an amazing group of people who make up my chosen family and friends, but I was still craving to belong, to be part of a community; I was simply craving my tribe.

In June 2022, I was presented with my first opportunity to engage with my community — well, at least the youth. I was asked to work at the Youth Services Pride Formal, being held as part of Pride Month celebrations. The Youth Services team is part of the organisation I worked for. I was specifically requested to attend as Carla. The team wanted the youth to know we came in all shapes and sizes. This was potentially going to be my first outing as Carla, so this came with its own level of excitement. In the lead-up to the event, the Youth Services team put a call out for donated formal wear, a post I shared with friends. I was overwhelmed when Bec contacted me and told me to come over to her home, as she had collected a few dresses. When I got there, her few dresses filled the back of my car. Her and her friends' generosity absolutely blew me away.

The night of the formal arrived, so I headed up to the Youth Centre after I finished in the office. While I had everything with me, I was still uncertain whether Carla would or could make an appearance. There was a screaming desire to be me, but I was also terrified. If I appeared as Carla, there would be no going back. I would be outed to many staff members, who were not across my shifting identity. With gentle encouragement from my cheer squad, I decided, got changed and emerged. I even let them put some makeup on me. I was so nervous, but I was buzzing. What a night. It was so good to see the kids being free to be themselves. Their smiles quickly washed all my fears away. I was in a safe place; they were in a safe place. Well, I thought at the time I was, until a few months later, when my attendance was used by a manager to try to accuse me of acting inappropriately and timesheet fraud. But that's another story.

Over the following few weeks, my confidence grew. Carla ventured out in public more frequently to a range of LGBTQIA+ events. But I was doing this solo; I was not with my tribe or even my family and friends. I had no one with whom to share these experiences. As such, the level of enjoyment rapidly faded. I think one of the contributing factors to the enjoyment fading is that I had to leave the house and return with no hint of Carla. The environment was toxic enough without adding fuel to the fire. Like with most things in life we don't enjoy, we stop doing them, and that's exactly what happened. Carla returned to the online presence predominantly. It was like taking five steps backwards. I was miserable and felt like I didn't belong in any world, let alone within the trans community.

In October 2022, I started planning activities for Transgender Awareness Week at work. During this planning, I realised that there were no Transgender Day of Remembrance (TDoR) events held in Wollongong. I didn't understand why and thought, Here is another chance to connect with my community. I hatched a plan to try to pull something together in the short time I had. I could find a small group from various organisations, who will support the idea. Unfortunately, I couldn't find people in the trans community who wanted to come together. What really sat me on my bottom was one response I got from a community member. They messaged me and said bluntly, *"We don't do things like that down here"*. While this was crushing to read, it spurred me on to try to build a community.

Fortunately, a voice in the dark reached out, and they suggested we do a TDoR stall at the upcoming Trans and Friends Festival. Initially, I was like, what would this look like? How would we translate a remembrance vigil into a stand? After the initial phone conversations with them, we met up. They were a ball of energy. They lit up, giving me hope. Before I knew it, I was neck deep in organising the stand with them. I don't really believe in fate, but I was also asked to take part in a panel discussion at the fair and read one of my poems, *Another Page*. From the low of the vigil idea failing, I was back on a high as I was being presented with multiple opportunities to engage with my community and foster my sense of belonging.

Chapter 7

Another Page

As the sun slowly rises in the east

The darkness of the night retreats

Its warm glow floods through the window

Rekindling the fire within

Prompting me to write another page

In this book of life

While many pages have been written already

16,000 and counting

Many of them have been turned over

Never to be read again

The story of my past is etched on my skin

By a means often unknown

The scars of time tell a story

A story of conflict, confusion, pain, and suffering

But those pages are from a time gone by

This story has sculpted me

It has made me who I am

It has shaped my mind

It has crafted my physical form

It has given me my heart

A heart that now beats to a new tune

I may not be a sculptural masterpiece,

But I am me, and that is enough

Almost a year has passed

Since the day I added the first page to this chapter

In that time, many things have changed

Many things have evolved

Treatments have commenced

Treatments that are helping to redefine myself

Much more is to come

As another page is added to the book of life

The latest pages talk about the power of acceptance

The power of love

The power of friendship

The pages have allowed me to be me

And accept who I am

They are empowering and all encompassing

I wrap myself in these words

Like the blanket that keeps me warm at night

While it's unclear how the pages will evolve

All I know is that they will

The pages will reflect a bright future

A future filled with hope

A future filled with love

A future filled with friendship and laughter

The warm glow of the sun will continue

Flooding my world

And illuminating my path,

Even when it is dark

Inspiring yet another page in the book of life

My new life

The day arrived, and I got to the university where the event was being held nice and early so that I could set up the stall and then get myself sorted. Given I was going to be setting up, I turned up very much in boy mode. I was at a point in my transition where boy mode was becoming very uncomfortable. It really made my skin crawl, but I couldn't do what I was doing if I was presenting as planned for the event. After finishing the setup, I quickly got changed and instantly felt more confident and comfortable in my skin. I ended up presenting super fem in a long black dress with a floral print and black heels. This stepped up even further when one girl at the event said, *"Come on, let's do your makeup."* It was the first time I had really worn makeup, and it was the icing on the cake. I was on top of the world, riding the euphoric high.

Despite the success of the day, I still didn't feel overly connected with my community. I still felt alone and isolated, like I was the only person going through this. Odd, I know, seeing how I had just spent the day surrounded by members of the trans community. I started thinking about what it is going to take for me to feel I belong, what's the barrier? When contemplating this, I realised it was a 'me' issue. I was really struggling with the dysphoria that living the hybrid life brought about. I think I was also still grappling with my identity and acceptance that I was trans, even though I was barrelling along with the hormone treatment. But more on the hormone treatment later in the book.

Chapter 7

In early January 2023, I was catching up with an online trans friend for the first time in person. While we were having coffee, I thought to myself; I wonder if I can bring the community together with an afternoon coffee meet-up. Before I knew it, I had tabled the idea and even spoken to the café owner about hosting it. All I wanted was a coffee and a face-to-face chat with members of my community. I floated the event on the local trans and non-binary Facebook group, expecting the same response that the TDoR idea got. I was silently praying that this would not be the case.

As the date approached, I found myself as an inpatient at South Coast Private Mental Hospital, more on that later, which made things trickier. After requesting permission to attend the event, I caught the train from Wollongong to Dapto, where the café was located. While the event had attracted many RSVP, I had learnt that this does not translate into attendance. I was very nervous that this was going to be a flop, and no one would show. While I sat in the café, the start time approached, and I was keeping myself company. My stress and anxiety levels climbed rapidly, given I am not good at waiting. To be fair, I think I will turn up at my funeral early. Slowly, people arrived, and within 30 minutes of the start time, 13 other members of my community surrounded me. Some had travelled over an hour to be there! As each person joined me, the anxiety I felt dissipated and was replaced with a euphoric high. My community was coming together. There are more of me out there, and we want to reach out and support each other.

For the next few hours, we sat drinking copious amounts of coffee, chatting freely and sharing stories. It was as if we had all known each other for years. Even the silent moments didn't feel uncomfortable. It was amazing. As we wrapped up, I floated the idea of making this a regular thing. While all in attendance were excited by the opportunity to catch up again, time would tell. I was bolstered by what had just happened, as I had achieved my goal. Now, to get it to be a self-sustaining event.

Two months is a long time to wait between drinks and test my coffee catch-up concept. I was even more nervous the second time around than I was the first. Was my idea a one-off success and die in the ditch, or does my community want to come together? Was this the avenue for that coming together? Like the previous catch-up, my anxiety was quickly replaced with excitement and that euphoric rush as familiar faces arrived. I think I could start breathing again. I was adamant that this idea to bring the community together really had legs. Like the first catch-up, the conversation just flowed as if we had all known each other for years. We even had a new face in the group. It was growing organically. Success.

Chapter 7

In my spare time, I am a member of the Illawarra Relay for Life organising committee. This is something that I have now done for over 10 years. Being involved in this group satisfies my innate desire to give back to the community and belief in swings and roundabouts, what goes around comes around. Specifically, if I am there supporting the community, when/if I need support, that support will be there. Typically, I would coordinate the work team entering the event. But this year, I organised a team from Rainbow South Coast for the 2023 event. I couldn't think of a better way to bring my rainbow community together while supporting another community group. Win - win in my world. When I floated the idea through my connections, I was amazed at the response I got. People were keen to get behind the idea. Based on this, Rainbow South Coast became one of the first teams registered for the 2023 event.

I love nothing more than bringing the community together and giving back. It's one thing that I hope my two girls will learn from me. Being part of a community is something special. Over the past few years, I have found my tribe and brought that community together. It has also been great as other members of my community build on these foundations and start putting other events on, such as a regular golf day. These successes made me smile. Life was good and, mostly, heading in the right direction.

Chapter 8

Tornado

---∞---

By November 2022, my world had fallen apart. The euphoria I'd felt since early 2022 was being replaced by feelings of loss and emptiness. My moods were increasingly unstable, high highs and low lows. My anxiety, depression, and dysphoric feelings were taking over my life. The scary part of it all was that I did not know. I was oblivious. I was blind to the impact that my instability was having on myself, my chosen family, and friends. I didn't want to hurt anyone; I had hurt enough people. The black dog was fighting back and winning.

The office gossip was in full force. I had people trying to contact me through various social media channels and even the work system. They either wanted to become friends or to ask questions. I had members of my inner circle telling me they were also being asked by random people from across the organisation. Ironically, those asking were all people who were mostly not even in any of my circles. I was informed that my manager was trying to find out information from others on the team and gossiping about me with other staff. I guess this was simply another reflection of his character and is precisely the reason I had said nothing to him.

For a while, I was distracted from office politics as it was Trans Awareness Week. A week to celebrate Trans Pride. A week for me to celebrate who I am and share that with my community. This week was so important to me, as it was my first. I buzzed that week, as I could organise for the Trans flag to be hoisted for the week outside the Administration Building. This had never occurred before. It was a first, and I felt immense pride as I watched it flapping in the wind. It was like the flag was waving at me, saying, 'You are valid, and you are recognised.' By Tuesday afternoon, and riding the wave of euphoria, I changed my name in the system at work. But I was not ready to do this. I did it to regain control and to stop the office gossip. Work now officially knew me as Carla. No more hiding behind the façade I had portrayed for the previous 15 years. Unbeknownst to me, the euphoric bubble was about to be burst…

On the following Thursday, I hit the wall, and I hit it hard. I was called into a meeting, which was presented as a welfare check-in, by the Director and one of the Senior Managers. The reality was that the meeting was an ambush. During the meeting, a raft of accusations was made against me, all of which were vexatious and not even remotely factual. This meeting was my last straw; I had been pushed too far. The office culture was toxic, and that toxicity was ingrained at all levels and across the organisation, from staff through to management. Following the meeting, I walked out of the office. I didn't know whether or when I would return.

Over the next few weeks, my moods were all over the place. I felt lost and alone. Days were spent either hiding in my room or spending time with Manda. I had met Manda while participating in acrobatics lessons. Manda is one of the most amazing, caring and loving people I have ever encountered in my life. She has a heart of gold and hugs to die for. Manda meant the world to me; we shared a connection that neither of us could explain — an intrinsic bond. Manda was my stabilising force; she was my enabler who encouraged me to be me, the real me. Her compassion, love, and support kept me stable. Well, more stable than I would have been without her. I was oblivious that the energy she was investing in supporting me was impacting her health. This was the last thing that I ever wanted.

Chapter 8

Unforeseen song

The distal sounds of a choir can be heard through the window of life

The infectious melodies reach deep into my soul

Demanding I listen

What is this new song?

It's unfamiliar

It's unforeseen

While at first the song is faint and hard to understand

The choir becomes louder and clearer

The clarity of the words opens my eyes, my heart and my mind

Like a flower unfurling and reaching for the sun

This unforeseen song cannot be ignored

It is a song of two

Two hearts that have just met but beat in tune

Two minds that align

Two smiles and two laughs

Two with a thirst for life

It's a song of a yet to be discovered journey

A journey into the unforeseen

As our paths have only just crossed

But these paths have become one

No longer are we just listening to the unforeseen song

Instead, we now sing as one

It is yet to be discovered how long our paths will merge

But hand in hand we will walk it together

Touching, listening, and feeling

Exploring this unforeseen world

Thriving in the sensory overload

And singing the unforeseen song

While the unforeseen song has only just begun

Many pages of the songbook remain unturned

And many lyrics are yet to be written

The choir of life beckons me to join in

It beckons us to join in

With Christmas approaching, my world was shaken to its core. Both my girls indicated that they were uncomfortable with how I was presenting and who I was becoming. Both requested that I no longer pick them up from school, attend school events or any social events where they may be seen with me. I was the parent who was always at the school carnival, discos, and other events, so this news crushed me. I felt like my heart had been ripped out of my chest, thrown to the ground and run over numerous times. I was devastated. Over the next few weeks, our relationship deteriorated rapidly. The deterioration was fuelled by their mother, who called me things like "freak" and "Bride of Frankenstein" in front of them. By Christmas, the relationship had completely crashed. I didn't even see them on Christmas Day. Something I now regret. These two girls gave me my reason to stay in the house, my reason to wake each morning, but now I was lost. They were lost to me.

Lost Girls

My girls are my life

they are why I breathe

I have lost them,

yet they are still here

Two lost girls

navigating the world without me

The loss of the parent they once knew

The person they loved and called Dad

How betrayed they must feel

Their lives upside down,

not knowing what to do

I don't know what to do

I miss their hugs

I miss their smiles

I miss them both,

my lost girls

Chapter 8

> With time they may be found
>
> With time, they may come back
>
> With time they may understand
>
> In the meantime
>
> I hope they remember,
>
> they are my girls
>
> and I will love them forever

A few days after Christmas, I packed my 4WD and headed to the Victorian High Country with mates from my 4WD Club. I'd been looking forward to this trip for such a long time, as I wanted to share this amazing part of Australia with my girls. But I was travelling solo, both girls declaring that they didn't want to come anymore. While I enjoyed the trip, it was emotionally challenging to know my girls were not there with me. I missed them and missed sharing one of my happy places. Maybe one day, I will get to share the high country with them.

Subconsciously, my mental health continued to decline. The downward spiral had sped up rapidly. My moods were more extreme, more volatile, and unstable. The highs were very high, and the lows, well; they were low. What made it worse was that I typically had no recollection of the highs or the lows. My head was spinning. I was out of control, flying headfirst towards a wall I could not yet see. The black dog had really sunk its teeth in.

Tornado

My thoughts are spinning
Like a tornado
Carving up the landscape
The howling winds
Echoing the noise in my mind

While my thoughts are loud
They are soothing
While my thoughts are chaotic
They are organised

Debris
Debris is everywhere
The remains of my old facade
Lay scattered at my feet

The gusting winds
The increasing noise
The debris flying violently
It fills my vision
It fills my thoughts
But all I see is calm

All I feel is peace

While the tornado was destructive

It has sorted the debris

In the same way a farmer

Separates the wheat from the chaff

Retaining only what is needed

Retaining only what is valuable

Retaining only the material I require

With this material

I build footings

Deep and strong

Cementing my heart

And stabilising my mind

I shape a new frame

A frame which suits my needs

A frame which is strong

Strong enough to withstand anything thrown at it

The frame is clad

In a material and style

Which truly reflects me

A style which affirms my identity

This is me

The chaos and noise of the tornado

Has reconstructed me

From the debris of my past

I am stronger than ever

I am proud

I am resolute

I am me

The Australia Day weekend arrived, and I headed for the bush again. Like previous trips, I left the day before, spending the first night alone at a truck stop, just to avoid being at the house. This was another trip that I was looking forward to spending time with my girls. But again, they declined to come. I found this particularly challenging as there were several families in attendance, and I was surrounded by young ladies of a similar age to my two. Even though I was surrounded by a great group of people and knew I had an amazing support network at home, I felt alone; I felt hollow and empty. I was alone in my soul-destroying darkness.

Alone

Alone is a dark place

An emptiness exists

Sucked into a black hole

Sucked into its vortex

While I drive the trails of my happy places

The passenger seats are empty

Like the hollow trees I pass

Burnt by fires past.

A hollowness persists

As I drive these trails alone.

Listening to the familiar voices

Of those swimming in the river below

The chatter of the adults

The squeal of the kids

The splash of the water

Surrounded by people who I know

I sit alone

Why do I feel alone?

I look to my left

I look to my right

I see couples

I see families

I see my reflection

I see myself alone

I have lost my girls

But hope they will return.

I have lost my house

But it was never a home.

I have lost my marriage

But is that really a loss?

I feel alone

Why does this loneliness exist?

I am surrounded by friends

And my chosen family

I am fighting the black dog

A battle I must win

I know who I am

The battle of identity is won

Or is it?

Is that why I feel alone?

Chapter 8

Alone is a dark place

The light still shines in the distance

So close, but so far

Fingers outstretched

And an open heart

Striving to reach the light

I don't want to feel alone

I cannot not feel alone

I had got to the point where I felt I was ready to return to work a few days a week. I dragged myself out of bed and got ready; I was in a good place. Yet, as I was driving in, I felt the anxiety building and the negative thoughts regarding my experience in the workplace returning. After dropping off my bag, I headed to have a coffee, which was my normal routine. I calmed myself and returned to the office. When I walked through the front door and sat at my desk, my body started trembling uncontrollably. I battled on until lunch, but I was done. The next day, I tried again and had a similar reaction. This place was really getting to me.

I felt the need to distance myself from Manda, given the impact I was having on her. I even went as far as telling her I wanted to fade her out of my life. Truth is, I wanted to hold her heart closer than I had in the past. I cherished what we had, but I just couldn't comprehend hurting her more than I had. I was scared; I was terrified, and my world was out of control. How out of control I would discover the very next day.

The day started great; I was on a high with a smile from ear to ear as I arrived at Manda's place. Manda's business was heading to the Nan Tien Temple Health and Wellbeing market. The day was a success from the moment we set up the stand. I love watching Manda do her thing. She is very passionate about her tea. Watching her thrive in this environment just made my smile bigger, my high higher. Her euphoria fuelled mine. But deep down, all was not well, and I was just blind to it.

That afternoon, I crashed. My mood plummeted, and I acknowledged to Manda how scared I was and how out of control I felt. I again expressed my regret for hurting her and explained my need to push her away, something I still did not want to do. Following our chat, I left. The drive home is a blur; it was like I was on autopilot. While I drove, the lights dimmed. How long before they turned off?

The roller coaster

As the coaster pulls into the station

And jolts to a stop

My head is full of emotions

The tears flowing free

Tears of loss

Tears of joy

The belts have loosened

The safety harness risen

The ride has ended

I rode this ride with one other person.

A special person

A person who entered my world

Like a whirlwind

From day one, it was strap in

And hang on tight

What an insane ride it's been

But an amazing one

The ups and the downs

The twists and the turns

The fast and the slow

And now no more

The ride was built on heart
A connection I cannot explain
A connection I do not understand
A deep connection
A connection that remains
Even though it looks different

People come and go through life
Some, for a short time
Some forever
But we ride for a reason
Why did we share this short ride?
That I do not truly know
I guess time will truly tell

The ride has ended
And I have alighted
While I wish the ride went on
It doesn't
I thank my ride partner
Who sat next to me for a while
And wish them true happiness
For when they next ride

Chapter 8

The garage door slowly ascended, and I was overcome with an odd feeling. A feeling that is hard to articulate other than I was present yet completely detached. The lights were on, but no one was home. As the garage door lowered behind me, I grabbed a short length of abseil rope and headed for my room, shutting and locking the door behind me. To this day, I don't know what prompted this action. In my room, I slowly and calmly unpacked my backpack and put my washing away before sitting on the end of the bed, tying the noose, and placing it around my neck. By this stage, I was crying but didn't know why. I published a post that said sorry to all my friends and asked for their forgiveness. Somewhere while this was all going on, a calmness descended. Everything was clear and emotionless. I had tied off the rope and have vague recollections of my phone constantly ringing. Then the lights went out, I gagged, then nothing. The final curtain had not eventuated; the anchor point had slipped. As I sat with my back against the door and the rope still tight, I hoped I would fall asleep, slump, and that would be that.

Final Curtain

Life is like a stage production

Full of characters

The good who make you smile

The average who you tolerate

And the painful who you wish didn't exist

The plot of life twists and turns

Like a road

As it climbs a mountain

Around each corner there is a surprise

Some good

Some bad

As the show goes on

The emotions fluctuate

Up and down

Up and down

In the same way a boat rides the swell

However, if the boat is not balanced

The boat will tip

So, hang on for the ride

Chapter 8

The lights dim

And the curtains slowly close

This marks the end

The show is done

While the show must go on for others

My show is feeling done

Bash, bash, bash. *"This is the police."* I was still attached to the anchor, so I told them I was okay and to leave me alone. They refused to leave until they set eyes on me. I quickly removed and hid the rope before opening the door just enough so that I could poke my head out. I spoke to them for a while, and then they left. I was so cranky that they had interrupted me and even crankier with the person who had called them. Once they left, I slumped against the door and stared vacantly into space.

The phone kept ringing. It was becoming irritating. I abruptly answered the phone, and it was Steph, a former student and now a long-time friend. She was the one who had called the police. She was the one who had interrupted the closing of the curtain. Throughout the conversation, I kept telling her she had overreacted, and nothing had happened or was going to happen. Eventually, and with very mixed feelings, I agreed to go to her place for the evening.

Steph greeted me in the driveway with a massive hug. While she hugged me, I cracked. I told her the truth. I had just tried and failed to end it all.

For once in my life, I had failed by doing something half-assed. Something my knowledge and experience should have prevented. Post the event, my friends have all said how grateful they are that I stuffed this up. My phone did not stop that evening, between calls and messages. My chosen family were all reaching out. The reality of what had occurred had set in. I was emotionally and physically exhausted. I felt like I could not deal with anymore, and my cup had more holes in it than a colander. Little did I know what the next few days would look like for me. I had opened a can of worms and set off a chain reaction that I was not in control of.

In the early hours of the morning, I had emailed my clinical psychologist and disclosed to her what had happened. I had planned to contact my GP on Monday. I guess I realised I needed help, and I wanted to see her. I was not expecting a response until the following Monday. But I was surprised to find an email from my psychologist later that day, informing me she had booked me in for an emergency appointment. I had also inadvertently emailed the psychiatrist I was paying to write a letter to say I was transgender, so I could access my Super. With this email, I would both celebrate and regret.

Chapter 8

Sunday morning, I lay in bed, debating if I should tell Manda. I didn't want to hurt her but also felt the need to be transparent. Something I had promised her I would be from the first day we met. I sent her a message: *"Please don't overthink or overreact to what is below. Last night, I tried and failed to end things. One of my friends called the police. I'm okay, and everything is fine. I don't want to tell you but felt the need to be open."* Within minutes of sending the message, Manda was on the phone to me. That conversation was one of the toughest conversations I have had in my life. I was terrified.

Following the chat, Manda and I caught up for lunch. I opened even more about how I felt and the impact I had on her. During the conversation, I suggested a walk, as I needed to stretch the legs. After initially suggesting Wollongong and Manda suggesting Minnamurra, we ended up at Loves Bay in Kiama, where I showed her the lava tubes. That afternoon, we spent eating ice cream and cuddling up to each other in the park. As special as it felt, I could not relax, reflecting on what had occurred and the ramifications. I had unintentionally hurt Manda, one of the most important people in my world.

The following day, Metallica's One playing full blast broke my slumber. It took a while for my brain to register what was going on; it was my phone ringing. In a dazed state, I answered. It was the GP's office telling me I had an hour to get into the office to see her. I knew it would be a challenge, but I tried. I knew I would be late, so called them to reschedule for later that day. Within minutes of this call, the receptionist called me back and said, keep coming.

On arrival, my GP was waiting, so I sheepishly entered her office. I felt like a schoolkid being sent to the principal for misbehaving. I was a closed book, with no desire to talk. I was angry. No, I was irate that I had been ordered to come in to see her. I was also stressing about how I was going to cover the costs, as I had been living week to week with nothing to spare for some time. This was compounded because I had to pay for my psychologist appointment later that day. For over an hour, I sat there as she tried to get me to discuss things. She kept suggesting that I needed to go to the hospital. She also told me that the psychiatrist would not support my accessing my super to fund surgery. Towards the end, my GP became very blunt. I was told in no uncertain circumstances that I was self-admitting to South Coast Private, a private mental health hospital in Wollongong, or she was going to section me under the Mental Health Act and then be forced into the public system. I had no choice; I took the lesser of the two evils and reluctantly agreed to the private hospital. The disappointment and frustration in her voice throughout the conversation were clear. But in hindsight, this was overprinted with concern and compassion. I was just too blind to see what was unfolding in front of me.

Later that day, I met with my psychologist. Initially, she indicated she didn't really think that hospitalisation would be required. Though as we continued to chat, she started telling me I needed to go to the hospital. I needed access to specialists who could dedicate the time required, a safe place, and a place to give me the space to breathe and heal. By the end of this conversation, I was confused, frustrated, scared and angry. I was going to be forced to go, forced to do something I didn't want to do. My thoughts again turned to how I could stuff up rigging something I historically did for a living. The rest of the day was spent waiting for the call to admit myself. But the call never came.

The following day, I begrudgingly headed to see my GP again as directed. All I could think about was wasting money I didn't have and time I didn't want to waste on me. I knew that if I didn't check in with her, she would call the police and have me sectioned, something I dreaded more than the concept of taking myself to hospital. As I drove in, I had decided that being who I am is too hard. I was going to stop. Being trans was just another façade I was trying to hide behind. I must have already been thinking along these lines prior to leaving, as I was dressed very masculinely. I don't think I had presented to Brooke that way in close to a year.

As with the previous morning, I was ushered into my GP's office, where I sat down, and she started talking to me again about what went on and where my head was at. It was at this point that I indicated I would no longer transition. I was not trans, and it's too hard. The position I had adopted annoyed her. She kept reminding me of how adamant I was about being Carla, to where I had outlined surgical plans the week before. I kept rebutting, telling her, it's not me. I am not trans. Eventually; my GP had heard enough and snapped. I was told in no uncertain terms that, in her opinion, I was behaving like a tantrum-throwing toddler. My frontal cortex had shut down, and the amygdala was running hot. Leaving the office with my tail between my legs, all I wanted was for all of this to end and to go back to how it was. Pretend this didn't happen. Avoid at all costs.

Slumping into the lounge at one of my favourite cafes, the analytical part of my brain functioned. What had I done, and what had I achieved? The initial thought was nothing other than creating problems for myself and others. It could have just been the many coffees, but I realised that this failed for a reason. Maybe something positive was to come of this experience. I guess time will tell.

Following the fall

The veil of darkness

Failed to fall

My head raced

My heart pounded

What had I done?

What was to come?

The phone rang incessantly

The messages flooded in

My family reached out

They took my hand

And held it tight

They took my heart

And held it close

The pain you feel

Will pass with time

The anger you feel

Clouds your thoughts

The red mist

Blinds you to the truth
Like driving through thick fog
The path ahead is unclear

You need help
Although you don't feel it
Although you don't see it
Although you don't deserve it
You have no choice
You go your way
Or you go my way
Your way is best

The rug has been pulled
You have no control
It's time
It's time to regain control
You deserve to thrive
You deserve to be you

Chapter 8

Now it's time to heal

Place a dressing on your heart

Place a dressing on your soul

It's time to move forward

But remember

Sometimes, you've got to fall

Before you fly

You have escaped the cage

You have survived the fall

So now spread your wings and fly

"Hello Carla, I am from South Coast Private, just ringing to advise we have a bed for you. Can you be here by 5 pm?" Reality hit home as I quickly finished coffee number 6. I was about to become an inmate — I mean, an inpatient. I had two hours to get my stuff sorted. Where is the money coming from? What to pack? How am I getting there? What to tell the girls? My head started racing. I was ready to tell them not to worry about it. I will delay the admission or tell my GP I self-admitted to Shellharbour and then checked out. Deep down, I knew this would not help me or anyone in my life. While I was still disgruntled and ensured everyone knew this, with the support of my chosen family, I had packed my bag and was on my way to the hospital. It was time to learn, time to understand and time to heal. I just didn't know that yet.

I was embarrassed by the events of the previous few days and didn't want my kids to know where I was. I simply told them I was going away for a bit. To help with the cover story, I left my car at Manda's place, and a mate dropped me in. Stepping through the front doors of the hospital was harder than I thought. What am I doing? I don't need to be here; these people do not know! On arrival, I completed the documents and had the mandatory COVID test before being ushered off to see the psychiatrist. All I could think about is

Chapter 8

'Who is the bloke?' and 'What is he going to do for me?' Just more time wasted...

"Carla, please come in." This was one of the softest yet warmest voices I had heard in a long time. Standing in the doorway was my psychiatrist, a slender, well-dressed man, gently urging me to come to his office for a chat. The soft nature of the Dr put me at ease, but I was still angry and had no plan to talk. During the conversation, my animosity was clear until the psychiatrist indicated my GP had revealed in the referral my reluctance to being admitted. I was told I would see him every day, and I could not leave the premises. This information agitated me more, but it didn't stop there. I was then taken to my room where my bag was searched, keys taken along with any cords and straps. I had just become an inmate at the prison. Well, that's how it felt.

That night, sleep was optional; I basically had none. I vividly remember seeing the clock tick over hour after hour. The insomnia was debilitating. But at some stage, after 4 am, I must have finally crashed only to be woken by the hospital GP wanting to talk to me at 10:30 am. I don't think I was that coherent or cooperative during that chat, because I was frustrated and exhausted. I am yet to see the point of the conversation, but I guess it's just a thing they did. The rest of that day was spent hiding in my room, trying to avoid the world.

With new sleeping meds on board, I had a much better sleep that night and woke feeling more optimistic about what was to come. I had realised that I mattered! I was valuable! I had something to contribute to the world! That I deserved to be here! There must be a reason for the attempt to have failed. These realisations made me more open to understanding and intrinsically more at peace with the situation I found myself in. In the following days, I continued to find my feet and feel more comfortable. So comfortable that I had taken up residency in the common area and started engaging with the other patients.

Little did I know that taking up residency would become a critical part of my healing, a critical part of my accepting who I am. Over the days, I had many conversations with other patients and staff about myself, my journey of discovery and what life is like for a trans person. I came to realise that I was probably the first trans person they had ever noticed, or more to the point, interacted with.

<u>7 DAYS</u>

7 days have passed

Since that fateful day,

The day my brain failed

The day it was nearly the end

The day of the final curtain

Attempted to draw closed

But…

7 days have passed

The healing has begun

A soft voice ushers me in

Sessions with supports

Has lifted the veil

Shown me hope

Reinforcing my value

7 days have passed

The light through my window

Is brighter than before

The path is clear

Lined in blue, pink and white

The light penetrates deep

The light warms my heart

7 days have passed

It's time to share

Share who I am

Celebrate who I am

Celebrate my family

Celebrate the compassion, love and hope

That I have to share

7 days have passed

Friendships have formed

Stories told

Even though they all differ

We have each other's backs

Chapter 8

A shared understanding

Cement the bonds

We all want to thrive

And we will

7 days have passed

I have realised

I am not alone

My chosen family is there

They hold my hand

They prop me up

Shelter me from the world

When I can not

A lot has happened the past 7 days

My world has been frenetic

It has been up and down

The tears have flowed

And the smiles grow large

On this ride

The roller coaster of life

The healing has begun

During my stint in the hospital, I made a lot of big decisions. One of the biggest decisions I made was to formally change my name. I had been very comfortable with my preferred first and middle names, but I was still undecided about changing my surname. I had been playing with changing it to Hope. I think the uncertainty was intrinsically linked to my girls having a different surname to me. My need to distance myself from my past won out, and I changed my surname. To my surprise, the formalisation of my name change occurred within a few days of submitting my application. I was now officially Carla Aurora Hope.

The longer I spent in the hospital, the easier life appeared to become. Several of the stressors that had triggered my major crash were resolved. I had worked through the challenges I was facing regarding my medical transition. My home loan application was approved, and I exchanged on a new property. I was adamant that this was to be a home, not a house. All was not as it seemed in that respect, but more on that later. The biggest stressor was getting formally diagnosed with a range of mental health conditions, such as autism, borderline personality disorder, and complex post-traumatic stress disorder. I now knew what I was fighting against. The removal of these stressors contributed to my being allowed to leave the hospital earlier than scheduled.

Chapter 8

The early release from the hospital was a massive moment in my life. It meant that I could take part in my first Mardi Gras. From the minute I arrived, I was on a euphoric high. What a sensory overload! What an eye-opening experience! I looked to my left and to my right and I realised people just like me surrounded me. I had found my tribe; I wasn't alone as I had felt. Click, click, click the parade had begun, and I switched to photography mode. The parade itself was a blur to me. I recall running around trying to capture my new family, but I couldn't tell you much more than that.

But all highs end. I crashed a few days later. My euphoria imploded, and I wished for it all to end again. I was back in the dark hole that had threatened to swallow me a few weeks earlier. But there was a difference; my time at the hospital had prepared me for the crash response. Enacting my plan saved the day. My family reached out, took my hand and my heart. They showed me that there was a point to this and that the hole I was in was temporary. There was much to live for.

What the hell am I thinking? I hate heights…

The very next day, I threw myself out of a perfectly good plane as part of the Wollongong World Pride Sky Dive. Jumping was a surreal experience. You know you're falling, but you do not know just how fast you are falling. The ground doesn't appear to get any closer. It's not until the parachute opened that I realised what had just happened.

The freedom, the rush — I was going to have to do it again. What I hadn't realised until watching the video, I had a wardrobe malfunction, which resulted in my breast falling out of my dress. Whoops… What an experience, what a rush. It got even better when I won the best dressed and got to jump again with a friend. My emotional rollercoaster ride continued.

Chapter 8

The Early Years

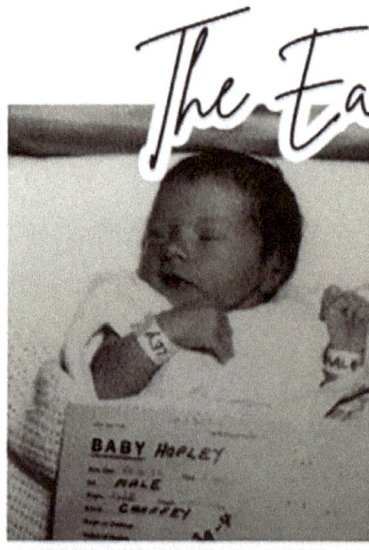

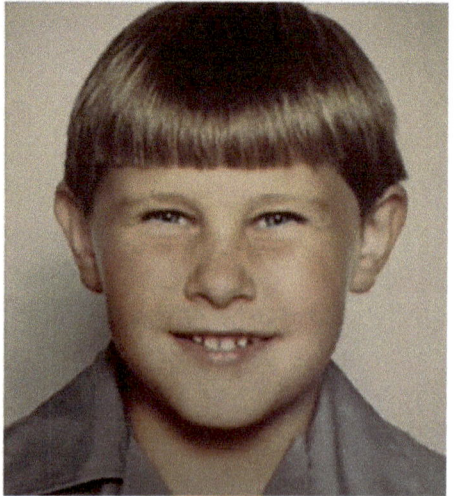

Behind the Facade

Chapter 8

Behind the Facade

Behind the Facade

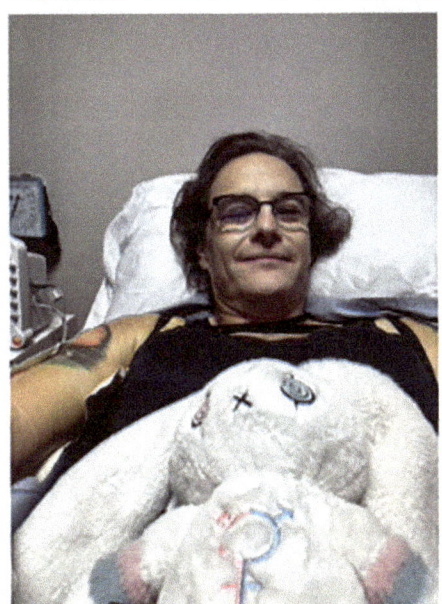

Chapter 8

Behind the Facade

Chapter 9

Home

―∞―

Joondalup Parkway never felt like a home to me. I know it was home to my girls, but it was a house to me. I have very mixed emotions about that place. I have so many happy memories because of the girls growing up. Conversely, I am haunted by the issues with the build and the toxic nature of what went on behind closed doors. I was glad when it was determined to sell the place.

Putting the place on the market meant work for me. It was expected that I would repaint the inside of the house, among other things. Like everything I did, it was never good enough. One wall got painted at least a dozen times. The wall was not perfect; you could see the joins in the gyprock, but it was my painting that kept being blamed for how it looked. To this day, I don't know why I persisted for so long. Maybe it was frustration with having to spend time and money on a place I hated, or the inner voice, which told me regularly I was not good enough. The more I think about it, it was a bit from column A and a bit from column B. While I hated painting; the backyard was a bigger issue. Ares had decided she didn't want grass but wanted gravel pathways and planted mounds. The real estate agent told us to remove all the gravel, etc., and return the area to grass. I was ropable as I never wanted to spend money, or the time, on these gravel paths, and now I had to undo it all.

Selling the house was a nightmare; the market crashed around our ears. We originally had the property listed for $2.3 million, but as time passed, the asking price plummeted. I'd had enough. I was ready to change agents, as I was not convinced that we were in the best hands. This is something that I still feel to this day, but it was the agent Ares wanted, so it's the agent we had. Eventually, an offer came in mid-January 2023, well below the asking price. By this point, I was so over it all and strongly recommended that we accept the offer so we could move on with our lives. We ended up selling for $450,000 below our original asking price. It was an insane amount of money to wave goodbye to but necessary for my survival.

While all of this was going on, I had been looking for a new house, somewhere to make my home. I originally started looking at large free-standing homes, as that's what I had convinced myself I needed. But was it really? Did I need a large home when, mostly, it was going to be just me? No matter how hard I tried to convince myself I didn't need a house, I kept looking at them. It wasn't until Manda convinced me to create a list of must have and nice-to-haves.

Chapter 9

My must-have list included garage/storage space, at least three good-sized bedrooms and an open plan. The nice to haves include things like a fourth bedroom, study, large kitchen, and walk-in wardrobe. I didn't need a house after all. This changed things significantly. I had now opened the possibility of a duplex.

With this wider scope, the hunt for a new home resumed, and the urgency increased as we had a proposed settlement date for the Shell Cove property. One morning, while looking at online listings, I found two potential properties. One was a new build, and the other was a two-year-old property. After inspecting the new build, I was disappointed with what it offered for the price they were asking. Was I wrong in thinking that a duplex would be suitable for me? I felt as if I had made a mistake. Later that day, I looked at a second duplex on a quiet street that backed onto bushland. When I pulled up, the street appeal immediately took me. The front façade caught my attention with its columns of reclaimed bricks and contrasting darker bricks. I loved the fact that there was no cladding, which would need maintenance down the track. Once the garage door slowly opened, I was hooked. Before me was a large open space and behind it a separate storage area. This was perfect, but what about the rest of the house? It was, after all, a two-year-old property. When I made it inside, it looked brand new. As I walked around the property, it ticked off more and more of my must-have list. I think I had found my home.

The following morning, I put in an offer on the property well below the asking price. I was trying to compensate for the low offer we had accepted on Joondalup. Not surprisingly, the offer was rejected by the owners. I put a second offer in, still below what they were asking. Not long after making the offer and without getting their response, I increased the offer. Crazy I know. But I wanted to secure this property. My gut told me I had found what felt like my forever home. This revised offer was accepted. I had got it; now to lock the finance in.

What was straightforward ended up being a painful experience that nearly cost me the property. Much of the issue was because of the debt that was carried over from the Joondalup property and Ares' personal debts. It took a long time to show, to the bank's satisfaction, that the debt was to be paid out on sale of the property, as the financial settlement documents were not signed off. After several weeks of negotiating with the bank, I secured the loan. Complicating the financial side of things, the purchasers of the Joondalup property refused to release the deposit so that I could use it to secure the new home. With the help of my conveyancer, I could lock in a deposit bond, which helped to resolve the issue. While all of this was going on, the owners of the

Chapter 9

property I was attempting to buy were trying to cancel the contract and put the property back on the market. My world was already spiralling; I didn't need this to fall through.

Over the following few weeks, I began slowly packing up what I was taking with me. I was putting over 20 years of my life into boxes and packing bags. Throughout this process, I continuously battled the black dog. This was harder than I had expected it to be. The exercise was shaking me to my core. What had I done? My mind took me to dark places where I didn't want to go. I was thinking, and it felt like I had made the biggest mistake of my life. Most nights, I cried myself to sleep as I slowly imploded. Packing the house got even harder when Ares told me she and the girls were moving out about two weeks prior to settlement.

I had lost my girls; they were gone. I missed waking to their chatter and seeing them each morning. Waking each morning in this giant empty house felt hollow. I didn't want to go on, but I had no choice. Packing continued at a snail's pace, and I was running out of time. I hadn't even started packing the two garages, which were full of camping equipment, tools, car parts, and the shell of my XM Falcon. I had to fabricate a dolly to mount the car so it could be moved to the new home. With days to go, I had no choice but to start on the garages. What a mission, but I got there in the end.

A few days out from moving, I did some work on my ute. It was a relatively straightforward job to replace the rear spring hangers. All I had to do was undo a few bolts, jack the car up, and swap out the hangers. But the 'best made plans' failed me. As I jacked the body away from the spring, the jack failed, causing the ute to come crashing down on me. I felt a massive impact on my knee and heard a pop. I knew I was in trouble. I was all alone with no one there to help me. I didn't realise at the time how much trouble I was in. I needed the ute to be on the road, so I dragged myself out from under it and found another jack, which allowed me to complete the job. By the time I had finished, my knee was massive, black/blue, and I was in agony. But I sucked it up, dismissing the injury.

A few days later, I went to the doctor, given that I was still in pain and struggling to walk. Maybe I had done some serious damage. When the Dr examined my knee, I got the look from her I occasionally get when I do something stupid. It's a look of *"What were you doing and why has it taken you this long to do something about it?"* During the consult, she made me an appointment to get an emergency MRI scan to determine exactly how much damage I had done. All I could think of was that I needed to move house in a few days. How was I going to do that when I could barely walk?

The results from the MRI were great. They showed I was consistent in that when I hurt myself; I do it well. I had ruptured my ACL to the point where it was not detectable in the scan. I had also damaged several other tendons in my knee. But this was not the complete picture. The force of the impact had caused internal shattering of the surrounding bones. No wonder I was in pain.

Despite this news, I had to push on. I had to be out of the house in two days' time. The next morning, I tackled a task I was dreading. I had to get the Falcon's shell loaded onto a car trailer ready for it to move to its new home. Everyone told me not to do it on my own, but I am both stubborn and determined. I was going to do it myself. After backing the trailer up to the garage door, the fun began. The trailer I had borrowed didn't have a winch fitted, so I had to improvise. I used my heavy-duty ratchet straps to drag the car up the ramp and onto the trailer. All was going according to plan until one ramp slipped off the trailer, causing the back of the car to shift sideways and precariously dangle half on and half off the trailer. I think I used the word that rhymes with truck many times as I surveyed the damage and tried to work out my recovery plan. Between jacks and straps, I recovered the car and got it onto the trailer. What I had hoped would be a straightforward exercise turned into a 5-hour slog.

Moving day arrived, and I was blessed that I had several friends turn up. Without them, there was no way I would have been able to move. I was completely useless. The transition had stripped me of my strength, and the knee injury was quite debilitating. While the removalists started emptying the house, my team of helpers started loading the small truck I'd hired with the contents of the garage. Amid all the loading, I had to leave and inspect the new property.

When I was returning to Joondalup Parkway, I got the call saying the removalists had left and were heading to my new place. But I had no keys, and the current owners refused to allow me access to the property until settlement had occurred, which was still two hours away. Pulling back up out of the front of the new home, I tried to work out what next. I didn't want to be paying for the removalists to be standing around doing nothing. To elevate the situation, I got them to unload and put the furniture either at the front or back door, based on where it had to go. Throughout this process, the removalists whinged they had to double-handle stuff. I ended up getting angry with them and reminded them that they were being paid by the hour, so they just needed to get on with it. I was so stressed by all that was going on around me. I'm just fortunate to have great mates who had my back.

Simultaneous settlement of the Joondalup and Whistlers Run properties happened at 2 pm. Yet as 2 pm approached, I started getting messages from my conveyancer, telling me that the system had crashed. What did this mean? Was I going to settle today? Here I was essentially homeless, with all my furniture sitting on the lawn outside what was my new home. My stress levels just kept climbing. All I could see was my world imploding, and all my doubts related to my transition, and the separation came rushing back. What the hell had I done? If it wasn't for two of my mates, I would have spiralled out of control. They kept reassuring me it would be okay.

2:30 pm arrived and went, the adjusted time for the revised settlement. But still no settlement. The system was still down. Stress levels kept climbing higher and higher. At one point, I walked away from everyone and had a cry. There was nothing I could do to make this all work. I was at the mercy of others. What made the situation worse was that the removalists were badgering me the whole time. I was really getting annoyed with them. I lost it and let them know what I really thought of them. I can assure you if I have to move again, I won't be calling them, nor would I recommend them to my worst enemy.

At 2:45, I got a message to say that the settlement had occurred. I could breathe again. My stress levels instantly decreased. Now, all I had to do was wait for the real estate agent to turn up and give me the keys. This was such a frustrating process. The instant I got the keys; I offloaded them to my best mate, who unlocked the house so that the furniture could be moved in. Feeling completely useless, I headed into the kitchen and started unpacking my new appliances, cutlery, and crockery. While I was doing this, my bedroom was being set up for me. At least I had somewhere to sleep and eat. Time to make the house my home.

I'm Home

They say home is where you lay your head to rest

Truth be told, that is not a home

That is a house for the lucky ones

Built of bricks and mortar

For 12 years I occupied a house

A house I designed

A house I helped to build

A house that was nothing more than a giant shell

A shell that projected an image of a success

A shell that overlooked a national park

A shell with ocean views

But that shell was never a home

The colours of the walls

The tiles in the bathroom

And the taps were all someone else's choice

The rooms were never big enough

And the main bathroom

Don't use that it may get dirty

The giant bath lay empty for 12 years
But it looked impressive
This was not a home

The day came when I closed the front door for the last time
With a thud it shut behind me
Like a clap of thunder resonating in a valley
The sound of the door echoed through the empty shell
I had left the house
With a dream to create a home
A home where I could be me
A home where the girls could be free

As one door closes another opens
Shell Cove was the past
Whistlers Run was the future
As I slid the key into the lock and turned it slowly
The familiar sound of a door opening was heard
I had just unlocked my door
The door to where I was planning on making a home

Chapter 9

Over the following days, I slowly unpacked. It was an overwhelming experience, and I spent many hours crying. I was restarting my life, and I didn't have the emotional skills I needed to cope. So many changes in such a short time. To make matters worse, I was due to travel to Argentina for the first of my surgeries. My world was out of control, and I was just hanging on.

While in Argentina, I had organised for my lounge to be recovered by a friend. The lounge had been around for well over 15 years and was looking tired, but structurally, it was in great shape. I also wanted to change it from the dark brown to a lighter colour to suit the new home. Returning from Argentina at the end of May, I discovered that the single seater and the three-seater lounge had been recovered. It looked great. I was so impressed with what she had done and couldn't wait for her to finish the job while I was in Thailand.

The two weeks I was back between returning from Argentina and flying to Thailand were a blur. I kept trying to do small things around the house to make it feel like a home. By this stage, I had accepted that I could do only so much in this short timeframe. I had to accept that I really needed to focus on healing rather than homemaking. The house would still be there when I got back from Thailand.

Me being me; I didn't stop. While overseas, I was ordering things for the new house. I wanted this to feel like my home as soon as possible. In the old house, my model car collection was not displayed. It was all packed in boxes and under the stairs. I was determined to resolve this and found a supplier of cabinets in Sydney. Based on their lead times, this would work out perfectly as they would be ready for installation the week that I got home. I was so happy as having the models on display after all those years was so important to me.

At the old house, I built an outdoor kitchen when we first moved, intending to add a pizza oven later. Yet, every time I went to buy a kit, there was always a reason we couldn't do it. Eventually, I gave up on that dream. It was just too hard. Now I had a new start. My dream was reborn, and I started searching for a kit to go into the new home. After looking into all my options, I found my dream kit and, even better; it was on sale with $1,000 off it. Bargain. I thought that these savings would be enough to cover the cost of the slab and other materials needed to assemble the oven. I was wrong... As with the display cabinets, the pizza oven would be ready for me when I returned from Thailand. Things were falling into place.

The surgery in Thailand took more out of me than I had expected. On my return, I went back into South Coast Private, as my doctors knew I wouldn't give myself the time I needed to recover. This three-week stay, while needed, delayed my homemaking that little bit longer. By now, I had owned the home for almost 6 months. It was difficult for me to wait out this time. I was so close, yet still so far from making the house a home.

Once out of hospital, I went on a mission. I had the cabinets delivered and set up on my second day home. All the models were on display by the end of the third day. Over the next week, I progressively installed my gallery hanging system so I could display my framed memorabilia. Like the models, these memorabilia had spent most of the time I had owned them in storage and not on display. These achievements filled my heart with joy. Another step closer. I was falling in love with my forever home.

With this task completed, I turned my attention to the pizza oven. It had arrived and was much larger than I had envisaged. Now, where to put it. Luckily, the top section of my retaining wall was the perfect working height for the oven. But there was a problem. The ground sloped up from the retaining wall. Out with the shovel and pick, I started excavating the hill. I was trying to eat my elephant, one bite at a time. But I found out that this was going to be tougher than expected. Post last surgery, my diminished strength, and endurance fell even further. I could only manage about an hour at a time before I would get too tired and needed to stop.

As I got close to finishing the excavation, my mind turned to the slab and retaining wall that I needed to build. I decided I would pour a slab and two nib walls to retain the soil. Though I'd never tackled either of these jobs, I convinced myself—how hard could it be? The more I investigated it, the more I realised it was beyond me. If I were to do it with cement bags, I calculated I would need over 100 bags. Too hard. Time to get quotes and a professional in to do the job.

The day arrived for the slab and walls to be poured. My notion of hiring a professional rapidly disappeared as a massive boom pump truck turned up two hours late and blocked the street. Let the circus begin. The two pump truck operators ran around in circles like headless chickens. It was so chaotic I had to laugh; otherwise, I would have been crying. Eventually, the concrete started flowing and filling the formwork. Then the concrete ran out, and the formwork was not full. No one had allowed for losses on the pump truck. After a quick call, more concrete was ordered and delivered. The job was finally done, but the circus continued. The operator of the pump truck took it upon themselves to pump the remaining concrete onto the next-door neighbour's block. 'Idiots' is all I can say… But I was home, and that's all that mattered to me.

While the display cabinets and the pizza oven were important, having the girls' rooms set up was even more important to me. When I purchased the property, I had them pick their respective rooms. I also asked them to find the furniture that they wanted for their rooms. Mili was straight on it and found the furniture that she wanted for her room. I ordered her bed and just had to wait for it to arrive. A trip to IKEA resulted in our finding the rest of her bedroom furniture plus other items for the home. We brought so much that the car was full; there was no more room for anything. I had even strapped some of the furniture boxes to the roof rack. Unlike Mili, Bel has yet to pick her furniture, so her room remains empty. I hope that one day soon, she will ask to fit out her room. When this day comes, I will be over the moon, as then I'll know both girls will have their rooms in our forever home.

Now that I have settled into my new home, I spend most afternoons sitting on the front veranda, watching the world go by as the sun sets, nibbling on cheese and biscuits. I'm loving my new life in my new home. I finally have a place that feels like home.

Chapter 10

The Physical Evolution

---∞---

When I looked in the mirror, all I could see was a mobile refrigerator staring back at me. Here I was at 150 kg, wearing 7XL shirts that were stretched tight over my arms and chest. All those hours in the gym had paid off. But no matter how big I was or how heavy I lifted, it was never enough. I had created an oversized hyper-masculine façade, my subconscious protective shell. In creating this shell, I had destroyed my health with unhealthy eating habits and consumption of supplements. I ended up with uncontrolled diabetes, blood pressure, and cholesterol issues. One of my first affirmations was that I was killing myself in more ways than one, and something needed to change before it was too late.

By mid-2021, I had made the decision that, for my benefit, and the benefit of my girls, the mobile refrigerator could be no more. My doctors were struggling to control my condition with medication. My physical health was spiralling, as was my mental health. I wanted to see my girls grow up, and the only way I could achieve this was to get my health in order. I actively changed my training and eating habits and focussed on dropping muscle mass and excess weight. Over six months, I dropped close to 30 kg. This drop on its own improved my physical health, but my mental health continued to decline. The mirror kept telling me I was a giant refrigerator. Why was I so uncomfortable in my skin? The level of physical dysphoria was increasing, and I didn't know why.

To gain control over my health, I reached out to my doctor and started investigating surgical options that could help manage my diabetes. These investigations led me to a surgeon in Sydney who was changing a bariatric procedure to help diabetics. I had to give it a go. I was sick of taking medications that were not working. I wanted my health back. This was my journey, and I was going to do it on my own. I didn't want my family involved. I was already building a wall between Ares and myself. Just before my birthday, I caught a train to Sydney and underwent the procedure. All went well, and I was released on my birthday. This surgery was a success and resulted in my diabetes going into remission, while my cholesterol and blood pressure returned to normal levels. As a bonus, I continued to drop size and lost nearly another 40 kg over the next 18 months.

Not long after accepting myself in early 2022, I felt the need to progress the physical transformation. My chief concern was doing it at a gradual pace, so I could sort my family life out. I also needed to do it in a way that I was comfortable. I have never liked how I looked. One of my pet peeves has always been body hair. I have never liked it and would often shave my legs when I was training with the excuse of taping my knees and ankles. I guess this could have been one of those early signs that I missed growing up. The last thing I wanted to deal with down the track was constant shaving. After asking some questions, I decided I would start getting laser.

Nervous excitement fuelled my first session. Everyone had said that it hurt, but to be honest, it was fine. I will admit that when she did my face, the top of my chest, and groin, I noticed it. I can honestly say that all dignity goes out the window when you get asked to drop your underwear and there is a stranger zapping you in the nether region. Two hours later and smelling of burnt hair, it was done. I had survived my first session and was so happy with the results.

While starting laser was a significant step, it really was just the beginning. I knew I had an extensive list of things that I wanted to happen, hoping that one day, I could look in the mirror and see someone that remotely resembled the person I feel I am. After doing some research, I made an appointment with my GP. Within the community, she had an excellent reputation, which put me at ease. On the day, I sheepishly entered her office. I was greeted with a bright, bubbly hello.

Chapter 10

I was nervous as 'all get up'. How do I tell a stranger that I am trans? I had accepted it only just myself. Irrespective of my nerves, I babbled on and eventually said the words, "*I think I am transgender, and I want to explore transition.*" I was very masculine-presenting and still tipped the scales at 120kg. There was very little femme about me, other than my resolve that my body did not match my heart and soul. Once I had muttered the words, her support was immediately clear. We discussed what had led me to this conclusion and worked out a plan to move forward under the informed consent model. At the end of the conversation, I was given a pathology form, which included a barrage of tests. I have seen shorter shopping lists, to be honest. My journey had begun, but I hadn't shared this with many people, not even my family. I was not that brave.

A few days later, I received my results. During the consultation, different options were presented, and I signed some paperwork, acknowledging that I was doing this under informed consent. Once I had signed the documents, I was handed the script for blockers. I was in shock that this was happening; my journey to being me had started. While I was in a daze, my GP was so happy and excited for me. She was bouncing around the room and talking about how she wished she had party poppers. It was a surreal experience, one where I still question whether my reaction was appropriate.

That afternoon, I had the script filled and held in my hand a box of Androcur 50mg and was to take half a tablet every second day. On the morning of February 18, I took my first dose and have not looked back. I was surprised at how quickly the blockers appeared to take effect. I noticed that some of my shirts, which were tight around my biceps, had loosened. My daughter commented that my arms looked skinny. Normally, a comment like this would frustrate me as my façade required me to be big and strong. However, now I smiled at her and said, *'Thank you.'* Her comment confirmed that my goal of decreasing muscle mass was working. I had dropped close to 15 kg in the first two months of being on the blocker. My body hair had also begun to soften and reduce. My body was feminising. I felt great; I was riding the euphoric wave. It was the first time I could remember feeling more comfortable in the shell I occupied.

Over the first few months, I became more emotional. I felt as though I cried a lot and developed a deeper need to try to understand who I am. I became fixated on trying to unpack my past to help me move forward. I do not know if this was the blocker or was just me not allowing myself to be me. I also noticed that I became calmer than I had ever been in the past. I felt it was near impossible to rattle. I guess one of the biggest mental changes I noticed related to self-care from a physical and mental health perspective. Historically, I would avoid doctors, but I found I became proactive in trying to understand what was going on with my body and the things I could do to look after myself.

At the start of April 2022, I had my checkup with my GP. A ball of energy and support greeted me as always. She instantly makes me smile. When I sat down, I handed her a packet of party poppers and commented on her celebratory comments at my last appointment. She took the party poppers and said Look what I have done since we last met, showing me her party jar. Our conversation turned to how I was going with the blockers. I discussed the loss of strength and bulk and the mood change. I also commented that many people noted they had not seen me so happy. She told me that my T levels had dropped significantly to 2.6, which is just above the typical female range. Whilst we were talking about changing the frequency of doses of the blocker, the topic of introducing estrogen (E) came up. I quickly said that I could start on my birthday, a day that I hate with a passion. I thought I could turn a negative into a positive. I will never forget when she said to me, "*You have already waited 44 years, why wait any longer?*"

As the conversations progressed, I mentioned the upcoming surgery to try to get me off the diabetes and lipid medications. These comments resulted in revisiting the conversation about starting E. I had hit a speed bump, which made my heart sink a little. My GP raised her concerns about the risks of starting E so close to surgery. All I heard in my head was *'No E for you'*, in the voice of the famous Soup Nazi in the Seinfeld series. She picked up on my mood change and started going through some documents with me about risks and outcomes. She asked me to go over the various options and get back to her a few weeks after surgery so we could look at getting the prescription sorted. The reality was, I just needed to wait four weeks post-op. While I was disappointed that the fleeting idea of a re-birthday was gone, I knew she only had my best interests at heart, and we would celebrate then.

On June 9, 2022, I had an appointment with my GP. As I walked from the carpark to the office, my heart was pounding. It was so bad I had to stop at the base of the stairs and regain composure. Not long after arriving, she called me in, and as she sat down, she noticed I was wearing a T-shirt that had more of a frilly sleeve. She commented that the top was different but really nice. This was the feminist I had presented. During the appointment, she informed me that the surgery had been a success, and that I was no longer classified as being a diabetic. She also told me that my lipids and other vitals were all back in the normal range. I was so happy with the information. At the appointment, she also gave me a flu shot, which she had to leave the room to get.

Chapter 10

On her return, she noticed the black boots that I was wearing and commented on how good they looked. Once the post-op and flu shot discussion ended, the mood changed.

My GP then started the next phase of the appointment by saying, *'Let's chat about the exciting stuff now.'* As we were chatting about how I was feeling from the perspective of transitioning, I didn't realise that she had typed up, printed, and signed a script for Estradot 50 patches (E). It was only when she lifted it off the desk and handed it to me that I realised this was happening; this was now real. The conversation continued for a further 20 minutes about starting on E. At the end of the chat, she took the script back and placed it in an envelope, to which she added several party poppers. I still have these with the date recorded on one of them.

With script in hand, I headed straight to Chemist Warehouse in Shellharbour to get it filled. I knew that even though I was not starting for a few days; I had to have the patches. This was an interesting experience. The chemist didn't bat an eye when I handed over the script. Though it became funny when the assistant didn't read the script properly and called out script for Carlie. She called it out several times before I realised it was probably my script. As I approached, she looked at me and then at the medication and went a little red. I was trying not to crack up.

In the lead-up to the appointment, I had decided that I wanted to share the moment I started HRT with someone special. I couldn't think of anyone better than Jen. Jen was one of the first at work to know about my transition and had been a pillar of support and knowledge sharing. In the lead-up to what would become known as E-Day, I sent her a cryptic message enquiring about how good her patch-sticking skills were. After a few more messages, where I actually requested that she apply the first patch, she was onboard, and we were both crying.

On June 14, 2022, Jen and I had lunch, where I had my standard Pad Gra Prow chicken hot 3. After lunch, we jumped in my ute and headed to the lighthouse overlooking Wollongong's south beach. At a little after one, I had started HRT (hormone replacement therapy); Jen had applied the first patch to my chest. I was on my way. Another step had been taken. At that moment, Jen and I embraced. I will never forget how that moment in time felt like. I just wish I had the words to describe the euphoria I felt. All I can say is I was buzzing. We sat down in silence, and I can remember sculling the glass of sparkling wine I had poured myself. Once I finished that one, I filled mine and topped up Jen's. I think we both sat and stared out towards the island to the south of us. Although we got so carried away at the time and didn't take a photo, every time I go to that spot and look upon that view, all I will remember is that moment in time. When my new life began. I think I will have to try to visit that site on June 14 every year.

While we were sitting there, we realised the time had gotten away and that the Pride Group meeting had started. I dialled in on my phone as we drove back to the office. Jen sent a message that she was having computer issues and would be late. I think we were a tad tipsy after drinking three quarters of a bottle so quickly and giggled like schoolgirls. If only the others in the group had any idea what was going on. What an amazing step my life had just taken.

The next six months were a rollercoaster of emotions as the hormones kicked in. My skin continued to soften, and my body hair reduced. I became even calmer than I had been before. I cried at the slightest thing, be it happy or sad. I quickly discovered my body was not responding well to the patches. The Estradiol levels in my body were not rising to the target range. By the end of six months, I had four patches stuck to my chest. I felt like an oversized post pack covered in stamps. Even with this higher dose, my levels failed to rise. Irrespective, my body continued to evolve. I had developed breast tissue and had reached a B cup by Christmas. Life was progressing. But how to address the hormone uptake issue? My GP's solution was to switch to implants. Little did I know that this issue was one stressor that led to my mental health spiralling out of control.

Chapter 11

The Argentinean Adventure

―――――――∞―――――――

Towards the end of 2022, I realised I wanted my medical transition to progress. I decided I wanted facial and body feminisation procedures. I had also decided that I wanted to undergo sexual reassignment surgery (SRS). I needed my body to look more feminine so that it matched my heart and soul. Being the researcher that I am, the hunt was on to find the surgical teams that met my needs. While it didn't take long for me to identify my preferred surgeons and start the conversations with them, it felt like an eternity. Prior to Christmas 2022, I had the doctors from the Facial Feminisation Centre in Argentina and Siam Transformations in Thailand on board. My medical transition just shifted into top gear and sped up forward. But how do I fund this? It's not going to be cheap by any stretch of the imagination.

The next step in the process was quite uncomfortable. I have never liked my body clothed, let alone fully naked. But I had no choice but to strip off and have photos taken from many weird and wonderful angles. It felt so wrong and unnatural for me to be doing it. What made it worse was that I was also required to measure my genitals. Despite the

Chapter 11

dysphoria that these events triggered, I could push forward, knowing it was a means to an end by getting my body to match who I am. Surgery dates were locked in, and it all became very real. My next challenge was how to fund the surgeries.

Once I received the quotes, my fears were realised. These surgeries were going to cost over $100,000. Where was that going to come from? Was this all a dream? By early January, I had applied for early release of superannuation under compassionate grounds. Dealing with the Australian Tax Office (ATO) is frustrating at the best of times, but my experience in getting access to my superannuation to fund the surgeries was infuriating. It took three attempts and several months before I received approval to release the funds. I was just fortunate that I spoke to a lady who understood and empathised. She did everything she could to guide me and to get the application approved. I will forever be indebted to her as she helped me to realise myself.

On April 10, 2023, my journey began with three flights from Sydney to Cordoba in Argentina. All I can say is I am grateful that I spent the extra money on flying business class. I got off the plane with minimal jet lag. The euphoria was high, but my mood quickly changed when I got to customs. I was detained and made to feel like I was a drug dealer. They had issues with the fact that I was carrying my medications, despite having a letter from my doctor itemising the medications and that I needed to take them whilst away. They also had an issue with my camera equipment and the drone I had purchased duty free. They wanted to confiscate those items or force me to pay Argentinian tax. It just felt so wrong and corrupt. In the end, I surrendered the drone and was told I could collect it when I flew back out in May. Paperwork completed, I headed for the terminal exit where I was to be picked up, but no one was around. I panicked and thought my driver had given up, as it was well over an hour since the plane had landed. To my relief, my driver appeared and greeted me warmly with, "*Ola, Ms Carla.*" I was tired and cranky at this point but relieved I was heading for my accommodation. Tomorrow was another day, and I had to focus on the big picture.

The next two days were mainly spent seeing doctors to get final pre-surgery clearances, though I could do some sightseeing in my downtime. Cordoba is an interesting mix of buildings and people. Our Lady of the Assumption Cathedral of Cordoba is breathtaking. It's hard to believe that construction began in 1582, with the current building completed in 1784. Externally, the building dominates the landscape, with its façade opening onto the Plaza San Martin, beckoning you inside. The other notable features are the enormous towers, central dome, and the statue of Christ the

Redeemer. As spectacular as the building's façade may be, it's only when you step inside and are engulfed by its grandeur that you truly see how spectacular it is. Internally, ornate gilded columns extend towards the ceiling, creating three distinct naves, with the central nave dominated by the cathedral's dome. The ceilings are beautifully decorated with frescos and sculptures extending back to the late 1700s. I was also fortunate enough to hear the angelic voices of the Cathedral choir echoing through the halls, begging me to sit quietly and recenter myself. It was an experience I will always remember. The skill and attention to detail of the craftspeople who worked on this structure are astonishing, surpassing today's standards. The white arcade of the cabildo (town council) building dominated the western side of the plaza, which, to my surprise, had the pride flag flying on one of its many flagpoles. Seeing the pride flag flying on such a historic building made my heart smile. Other key features include the central San Martin monument, the large flagpole, cobbled paving, and stunning green space. Cordoba is a beautiful city where its heritage is integrated into the present.

Beep, beep, beep — my alarm was telling me to wake up and get ready. Today is April 13, the day of my first surgery. With much excitement, I prepared myself for the day ahead. After being picked up on that cold, wet morning in the dark,

I was warmly welcomed at the hospital. The surgeon greeted me and got straight to work, marking me up with his Sharpie markers. I felt like a human sketchpad. Not long after, I walked into the operating room where I would spend the next 7 hours. This first surgery was about body feminisation. It included excess skin removal; approximately 5kg was removed; breast implants and buttock implants. The surgeon wanted to do fat transfers but could not find enough fat in my body, so I guess my weight loss journey had ended…

Post-surgery, several amazing ladies who stayed with me at my apartment looked after me. I had two favourites. One was like that stereotypical mother, who knew what you really needed before you did. Something I had missed growing up. The other was a different kettle of fish from my adopted mother. She was closer to my age, and we just hit it off from the moment we met. Even though most of our communication was via Google Translate and hand signals, we laughed so much; we got each other. I felt so loved and cared for during this time. I felt safe. The first night in the apartment on my own was a tough one. I didn't sleep that night and couldn't stop crying. I missed the company and the safety blanket, knowing that I had someone should I need them.

The next few weeks were spent recovering, wrapped in compression garments, feeling like a trussed-up chicken

Chapter 11

ready for the oven. But I was on such a euphoric high, the discomfort didn't bother me at all. The medical team kept telling me they were astounded at the rate of my recovery. The only hiccup I had was a large hematoma on one of my legs. The presence of the hematoma didn't bother me; I thought it was fascinating to see the upper portion of my left leg take on all kinds of shades of dark purple and black. What was even more entertaining was when it broke up, and I had to massage that part of the leg. It was a bit like a scene from a horror movie as I would push the fluid towards the drain incision, and it squirted out as a continuous stream. My leg had developed a fountain, which I controlled. After a week, it appeared to be getting better. But no, it wasn't. Because of the pressure buildup, the stitches failed at the junction of the two incisions, and I ended up with a large hole in my leg. Gross, hey, but cool Ha-Ha. Between my two surgeons, I was in expert hands. The treatment I received was second to none — well, so I thought.

While recovering from the body surgery, my medical team organised a few days away out of the city. These few days were a bit of a rollercoaster emotionally for me. I was excited to be getting away and into the mountains, but nervous as I had had no control over where I was going. I also knew I was limited in what I could physically do. The drive to Pueblo Nativo, where I stayed, was an interesting experience. I don't do passenger well at home, let alone sitting on what was the wrong side of the car and being driven by someone whose driving style I would describe as erratic. I am yet to work out what, if any, road rules exist in Argentina? At one point, we were doing just under 150 km/h in a zone, which I think was 130 km/h. While the speed was okay, it was cool being in a car at that speed again, although the random lane changes in this little Fiat were my greatest concern. Irrespective of everything else, the drive through the mountain range was spectacular. I had visions of driving it myself, under closed conditions at speed. I guess you can take the boy out of the rally driver but not the girl... Given I am here writing this; I guess I made it to my destination and back.

As we drove up the final gravel road, a large burgundy coloured building greeted me that, from the front, had been integrated into the topography seamlessly. Architecturally, it was spectacular, as much of the building was below the visible ground level. At check-in, I realised that this was going to be a struggle. It was the first time that the language barrier had become so overt. No one even spoke broken English. Later that night, I emotionally crashed and spiralled a bit. In hindsight, it was because I had stopped, and the enormity of everything going on smacked me across the face like a wet fish. It stank, it was slimy, and I'm allergic to fish,

Chapter 11

so not a pleasant experience. If it wasn't for my cheer squad back home, I would not have been able to drag myself out of the hole so quickly. I'm blessed to have such an amazing group of people by my side, holding my heart and hand while I embarked on this journey.

My downtime between doctors' appointments was spent wandering the streets of Cordoba. I will admit it's a beautiful city and hard to believe that some buildings are over 400 years old. Some might say I'm a bit of a coffee snob; well, who am I to argue… Anyway, whilst admiring the architecture, I was also focussed on finding coffee shops that would meet my needs. Yes, coffee to me is a need, not a want. It didn't take me long to find a few places that would become my home away from home cafés/restaurants. Giuseppe's was my favourite place to get my morning coffee. It was a quaint American styled café about a block away from where I was staying. After a few days, they knew my name and my order. The barista and I would have a chat in broken English and dodgy Spanish. Despite our language barrier, we both knew what we were talking about and had a good laugh. My afternoon coffee would typically be at Europea, a European styled bakery opened since 1887. While the coffee was good, the pastries were to die for. Because of the bakery, I never really got to know any of the staff, as they were always different except for one young lady. She always greeted me with a smile. El Quijole became my regular for dinner and my evening coffees. Wow, I really have a coffee issue... I had my favourite waitperson at El Quijole as well. Even though she didn't speak any English, we communicated brilliantly. Thank goodness for Google Translate.

Mirror, mirror

Mirror, mirror

Who is looking at me?

I'm the size of a fridge

Barrel chest and bulging arms

Scales screaming "Get off"

150kg and growing

Hyper masculine, big and strong

Ready for the unforeseen battle

I was what I wanted

Or so I thought

My skin crawled

Itchy, like that uncomfortable woollen jumper

Is this really me?

Am I a fridge with legs?

Why is my health so bad?

Why am I killing myself?

Behind the Facade

This obsessive training

And eating for a family

Had me self-destructing

I need to stop

I need to be well

My girls need me

And I them

Mirror, mirror

Why do you lie?

This image you reflect

Is nothing more than a façade

As time passes

The reflection it shifts

The façade is deconstructed

The old shirts hang like sacks

The barrel chest is no more

But the mind still lies

It sees the fridge staring back at me

Chapter 11

Why is this so?

The scales of time do not lie

I have changed

I am transitioning

Becoming increasingly me

Dysphoria was eating me alive

It was devouring me as a lion eats its prey

But a person less I was

While 60kg had gone

My skin still crawled

Mirror, mirror what is next?

Your body shell has shifted

But is still not you.

Where are the curves?

The femininity alludes you

Time for a change

Time to metamorphose

Behind the Facade

Mirror, mirror what do you see?

The fridge is no more looking back at me.

I see a shape that's more reflective of me

A softness of femininity is upon me

The mirror no longer lies

I'm freed from the past

This is me as far as the world can see

While more is to come

The mirror will reflect

Femininity not masculinity

The body metamorphosis is nearing its end

The shackles of history are broken

And the façade is down

Life has begun

This is me

And I'm Carla

Chapter 11

The day my face was to change arrived. With nervous excitement, I was picked up early from my accommodation and taken to the hospital. On arrival, my surgeon was waiting with his kit bag of texters. Here we go again. I was about to become a human canvas for my Mr Squiggle. In the back of my mind, I had the voice of Blackboard, from Mr Squiggle the kids TV show, telling the surgeon to *"Hurry up,"* while simultaneously hoping that I would not hear my Mr Squiggle utter the famous words, *"Upside down, Miss Jane…"* Not long after the drawing session was completed, I was taken back to that familiar theatre where the magic was going to happen. Several hours later, a very dazed and confused version of me recalls the blood being washed out of my hair, wrapped in bandages, and then being transferred to my room for the night. All was good. I had made it through another surgery, well, so I thought…

At some point, I regained consciousness in absolute panic. I felt like I was being suffocated and had subconscious flashbacks to the night where I tried to hang myself. I realised I was getting a blood infusion and had IV lines and oxygen nasal lines. I recall trying to tell the nurse that she had to get all the bandages off me and remove all the lines. As she didn't understand me, she panicked, which fed my panic. I had a full-blown overload; my brain was full and just not coping. The last thing I recall is being sedated.

The following few days are a blurry haze. I do not know how I got from the hospital to the apartment, but apparently, I slept all the way. Whatever they were sedating me with was working. I was a space cadet, but my mood was low as I came to. I was not in a good place. I felt trapped; I felt like nothing had changed, and I had made a mistake. The stitches and tape swelled and irritated my eyes, and I was black and blue with a tinge of yellow. I looked like I had tackled a truck, and the truck had won. The mirror was not my friend as I couldn't see beyond the mess my face was in. I could not see what was behind the façade. If it weren't for my two favourite nurses, I don't know how I would have coped. I crashed hard. These amazing ladies took my hands, held them tight, and reassured me I was okay; everything was going to be alright.

Chapter 11

The Face of Things

The face is said to be like a window
The window to our soul
Over the years, the view evolves
It tells a story
The pages of history etched on my face
Like the deep creases and cracks of my favourite leather boots

It's a story of mixed feelings
It's a face that has cried
A face that has smiled
At the face of things
Not too dissimilar to others
But also, not the same

The face concealed a deeper story
A story coded in my DNA
But this face did not tell the truth
It projected a lie
This was the face of another
A face that did not match
The heart and sole

12,000km from home

The face of things changed

A talented team took my face

A team who cared

A team who loved

A team who knew what lay concealed

Unlocking the truth

The face was bound tight

Suffocating me like the rope that night

I was black and blue

Swollen like a puffer fish

My brain freaked out

It couldn't cope

Was this a mistake?

What had I done?

That same team took my hand

They took my heart

They told me it will be all right

My Argentinian family had me

They held me tight

Chapter 11

While many of the stories of time

Have been smoothed

Blended into the background

They will no longer be seen

But will never be forgotten

The face tells a new story

The story that has laid dormant for 46 years

New storylines will evolve

And be etched as time passes

These will be my true storylines

Carla's lines

Over the period of a week, the swelling subsided. The bandages and stitches were all progressively removed. With each passing day, I could see a new version of myself. I was the same but very different. But dysphoria was still biting hard. My mood continued to fluctuate erratically. One day, I was fine; the next, I was telling the doctors that I felt I had wasted my money. My head was all over the place. I was uncomfortable, and at one point, I didn't sleep for 36 hours. I was a long way from home and felt very alone. All I can say is thank goodness for technology. A few calls home and chats over messenger, and my mood stabilised. I just need to stop, slow down and remember to breathe. I was reinventing myself, and I needed to recognise that my brain was going to have to play catch-up with the shifting façade.

The hurry and wait were over. My last surgery in Argentina had arrived! This was going to be the simplest of the surgeries to date. That morning, my driver whisked me off to the clinic. On arrival, my surgeon and her team were waiting for me and greeted me with a *"Hello Carla, ready for today?"* Today was the day my hairline would be changed forever. Gone would be the receding hairline, and it would be replaced with a new curved feminine hairline. The day started with the back of my head being shaved, which was a triggering experience, as my hair hadn't been cut for nearly two years. But I had to realise that this hair will grow back, something the hair on my temple would never do. The first four hours while the donation follicles were taken was a blur, courtesy of a sedation serum. The rest of the day was an interesting experience while thousands of holes were punched into my forehead, and three skilled hands strategically placed the harvested hair. After eight hours, the job was done, and I was escorted back to my accommodation to recover for the next few days.

Chapter 11

My Argentinian rollercoaster ride was almost at an end. The day before flying home, I experienced one of the most humbling and beautiful experiences of my trip to date. My sister from another mother, Mely, who had taken such great care of me, invited me to her home, where I shared a traditional home-cooked Argentinian BBQ lunch with her, her son, parents, and my surgeon. This experience resulted in my body being flooded with emotion. I was torn as I was glad to be heading home but extremely sad that I was going to be saying goodbye to my new family, my Argentinian family. I never expected to build such strong relationships with my medical team, let alone anyone else. But I was wrong. I found a local café, which became my regular, my home away from home café. Every morning, the barista, and the rest of the team welcomed me with open arms. It got to the point where I didn't need to order; they knew what I wanted. I will forever miss my extended family. But saying goodbye to my unexpected family made me cry. My new family will never know how special they are to me, what a difference they have made in my life. I have lived and loved my Argentinian rollercoaster. A ride I will always cherish.

Argentinian Rollercoaster

Wow, what a ride

Many ups and downs

My life has changed for ever

Both physically and mentally

My Argentinian rollercoaster

A ride I thought would end before it started

Hurdles getting funds released

Detained at the airport

Not knowing my address

And having my camera gear

Gear I had to surrender

Gear I prayed I'd get back

Released to an empty airport

Who was picking me up?

What would I do?

Madly rushed through the unfamiliar streets

To my first night's rest

Rest I needed!

Chapter 11

My brain was racing

My heart was pounding

What am I doing?

A voice deep inside said

I was doing what I needed to do to be me

This is about you being your true self

It's time for you to emerge

The first meeting with Dr Torres

Was a blur of mixed feelings

Excitement and nerves rolled into one

Like climbing the first hill on a coaster

A few days later, the coaster crested

The ride had begun

Rapidly, the momentum built

Marked up for surgery

My body was never to be the same again.

The excess skin, remains of the old facade

Deleted from my body

Replaced with taut skin and feminine curves

I had breasts, a bottom, and a waist.

The rush of excitement of closing the fridge door

I was on my way.

The facade had started its metamorphosis.

It started to match my heart and soul

The true me.

The surgery went well

Pain and relatively complication free

If it weren't for the large hematoma, all would have been perfect

But the Facial Feminisation team, my family, managed it to a T

My chosen family had grown

Emilio and Gabi, my two surgeons

Fabi, my Argentinian mother

Mely, my Argentinian sister

Ani, with her magic hands

You all took my hand and heart

You will all occupy a special place in it forever

Chapter 11

The ride was far from over

More was to come

Next was my face

My window to the world

The part of me most first see

The list of procedures grew

I trusted my team

I trusted they knew what I needed to be me

For the world to see the real me

Left and right and left again

Thrust violently through the curves

My mental state was all over the place

As I came out of sedation, I panicked

Gestures to remove all of the drips and cables helping me survive

Remove the bandages that felt like they were strangling me

My family stood by my side and got me through

Family dinners followed

It's not often you can say you we're having dinner with your medical team

Even invited to their home
These strangers no more
Families for sure

It was getting hard
As I knew the ride was almost at an end
My family extended beyond my medical team
Giuseppe Cafe became my second home
Greeted with a smile and a friendly Hola
They knew me and I them
They knew my order without me asking
Augustin, the barista, and I would chat
This meant the world to me
Another extension of my Argentinian family

The day of the final surgery arrived
Following a sleepless night
I was whisked off to the familiar clinic
Greeted by Gabi, I felt at ease
Eight hours later, my hairline had changed
Goodbye, the receding hairline
Hello, the feminine roundness!

Up and down through small rollers

My emotions fluctuated

The loss of hair from the back of my head was triggering

But it was for a purpose

It would return with time

While the loss was for now

The gain was permanent

The Argentinian rollercoaster was coming to an end

An end I both desired and dread

The outcomes have been achieved

I feel more like me

But saying goodbye to my unexpected family

Was hard and made me cry for the loss

I have lived and loved my Argentinian rollercoaster

A ride I will always cherish

A ride that has helped shape me

Chapter 12

The Stopover

To prepare for departure from Córdoba, I had an appointment where all the remaining stitches were removed. This included the removal of stitches from my glute implant site. Nearly two months after they were placed. Following their removal, I complained to the doctors that my glutes felt sore, and I was stiff. These comments were dismissed, saying that nothing was wrong with the implants and my glutes. While I was not convinced that nothing was wrong, I had to take their advice. They are the experts.

By the time I landed in Chili from Cordoba, I knew I had an issue. The back of my pants felt damp but not damp from sweat. During the stopover, I checked my clothes and noticed a stain on the back of them. After getting over the embarrassment from the realisation I was walking around with clothing that looked like I had soiled myself, I stressed. The stain lined up with the top of my bottom. While in the bathroom, I felt the glute incision site, and it didn't feel right. It felt soft, but as I don't have eyes in the back of my head, nor am I that flexible, I couldn't confirm if the incision had split. I was deflated. Besides having to manage the residual hole in my groin from the April surgery, I now had to deal with potential issues with the glute implants. I would just have to manage the situation until I got to see my doctor the following Thursday. My initial positive thoughts about my Argentinian adventure were gone. I was now confused and torn.

Me being me; I had prescheduled my two weeks stopover. I had booked my appointments and knew that I would have very little downtime. Even though I was stressed about the issues I was bringing back with me, I was on a euphoric high. I felt great, like I could take on the world. I finally felt that I could walk into any situation and not be clocked. The first evening was spent catching up with my best mate. It was an interesting experience, as he was taken aback, and I would see him trying to take in the changes. I guess it would be a lot when you have known this hyper-masculine guy for 40-odd years and now, you're looking at a much slender, feminine version of that same person.

Visits took up the next few days with my psychiatrist, catching up over coffee, as well as writing a job application. I had spotted this opportunity to change work teams when I landed back in Australia, but the application closed the same evening I arrived. I emailed the work recruitment team and was granted an extension. Even though I was jetlagged and not feeling 100%, I pushed on and got the application completed by the due time. Well, that's what I had thought. When I went to upload the application, the system told me it was closed. What the… I had completed it on time. As a last resort, I emailed the manager with my application and requested that it be considered. She responded to say it would be considered, as the system should have allowed me to upload. I hoped I would be successful, as I needed to get out of the toxic work team I was on. I was surprised when, a few weeks later, I received a call inviting me for an interview. An interview I ended up doing from my bed in Thailand, while I recovered from my gender reassignment surgery. While I felt comfortable in the interview, I also felt that I would not get the position. Which I didn't.

Friends from the Relay for Life Committee reached out and asked me to join them at the Cancer Council Dancing with the Stars event. This event is one of the major fundraisers for the Cancer Council. It was also a great opportunity to head out for a fun evening with friends. The event's timing was also ideal, falling between my Argentina and Thailand trips. I also wanted to thank my bestie for all she had done in Argentina, so I invited her to join me. I was amazed when she accepted my invitation. This night was going to be special, a night to remember.

Given this was going to be a gala event and, in some ways, my big reveal, I had to work out so many things, from what to wear to hair and makeup. This was a whole new world for me. All I can say is thank goodness for downtime and online shopping. Whilst in Argentina, I found a dress I liked. Because of my lack of confidence, thanks dysphoria, I shared the image of the dress with a few of my closest friends, asking their opinion. With unanimous support, I rolled the dice and ordered the dress. Now, I just had to pray it would fit and look as good as it did online.

The next piece of the puzzle was how I would present myself. My hair was shaved at the back because of the hair transplant and was not even that long. I was self-conscious about being able to pull this off. I reached out to my friends, and they took my hand. My beautician, Laura, reassured me and said she would get it sorted. I instantly felt comfortable. She had been by my side for 12 months, sharing my rollercoaster and watching the evolution of Carla. She had introduced me to others, who welcomed me with open arms and inflated my tyres when they were flat. She grounded me throughout the process, reminding me why I was doing this. Between her and her team, they made me feel me.

As Laura took my hand, she said to me, *"This is going to be your big reveal, your time to shine, and scream 'I am Carla!'. Trust me, and we will make your inner beauty shine on the outside."* These words made my eyes well up. I felt truly special. By the time we had finished our message exchanges, I was booked in for the works. Hair extensions, foils, colour, wax, nails, spray tan and even possibly the kitchen sink… The original plan was to spread this out over a few days.

One of the first things I did when I got home from Argentina was try on the new dress I ordered. I was stressed about how it would fit and look. Would I just look silly? Like I was trying too hard? With people saying, "Look at that guy in a dress?" When I first tried the dress on, I didn't know how I felt about it. Truthfully, I didn't like it on me, the fit or the colour. But I couldn't be sure if this was factual or my dysphoria was kicking in and driving my self-doubt. Seeking a second opinion, I took some selfies and sent them to my bestie, as I didn't want her to be embarrassed by how I looked. Within a few minutes, she came back to me, saying how good it looked and made a few suggestions re accessories. 'Take that dysphoria', you just lost this round.

I have always had a love-hate relationship with hair. I used my hair to help project my façade. Growing up, it was always short, to project a masculine façade. But now my hair and its link to identity were stronger than ever. Even though I had been growing my hair for nearly two years, it was still short and not what I perceived as feminine. Conversely, the hair growth on the rest of my body, particularly my face, was doing my head in. While laser had been doing its job, the two-month break from electrolysis showed. My electrolysis tech came to my rescue and squeezed me in several times that week. By Friday, my face was under control, as was my dysphoria associated with it.

Thursday became 'Crazy Day'. I was originally planning for it to be busy, but not as crazy as it became. After seeing my GP in the morning, she wanted me back the following day. She was uncomfortable with the state I had returned from Argentina in. The sad thing was she did not know about the hole in my leg; we hadn't got that far into the issues I was having. While in her office, I was transferred across to the nurses' room, where they packed the wound in my bottom and also took swabs checking for signs of infection. During that appointment, my GP suggested that the trip to Thailand might need to be cancelled. This was stressful, as I had everything planned out to the day. The suggestion of not going caused my mind to implode. What made it even worse was when she told me I was to go back the following day and see her. This really impacted my ability to get ready for the ball on Saturday, like I had planned.

Thankfully, Laura, came to my rescue and reorganised my appointments so that her team could get me prepped for the ball on Thursday. I did not know the whirlwind that was about to unfold. After walking in the door at 11 am, the team got to work straightaway. I was whisked off to the back room where my eyelashes and brows were sorted. Once that was done, I was then in the hairdressing hot seat. This was a surreal experience as the girls covered my head with foils. By the time they were done, I would have made a great lightning rod if I had walked outside in a lightning storm. But there was no time for that to happen. While the colour was in my hair, one of the other girls on the team was doing my nails. From nails, I went back to the hairdressing chair. It was feeling like I was in a game of musical chairs. From there, it was back for a pedicure, prior to my hair extensions being put in, and the day ending with a spray tan. Eight hours later, I emerged looking and feeling great. I think the biggest shift in my mentality was because of the hair extensions, which transformed my face and overall appearance. Dysphoria had just received another kick in the stomach. All the work that Laura and her team put in made me feel complete, made me feel me. It was now black and white; I looked and felt feminine.

The following day, I attended my GP's surgery. She was even more concerned about my health and the issues I was having following my Argentinian surgeries. On arrival, I was ushered into the nurse's room where the wound in my buttocks was re-examined. During the examination, the nurse thought that she could see something at the base of one tunnel but was unsure of what she could see. I found out later on that what she could see was one implant. It was not where it should have been. As the examination went on, the nurse

Chapter 12

and my GP looked at the hole in my groin that had been there for two months. It was at this point my worst nightmare was announced… in her opinion; I needed to go to hospital straight away, and I shouldn't go to Thailand the following week. Boom, my world crashed around my ankles. I skulked out of the surgery and headed to the hospital.

On arrival at the hospital, a very full waiting room. I knew I was in for a long wait. I started messaging my contact in Thailand to update her on what was going on. Over the next few hours, messages flowed back and forth between us. I had suggested that the surgery would need to be postponed, based on the advice from my GP. Unbeknownst to me, my Thai contact had been chatting with the surgeon at the same time as we were messaging each other. After I sent her the photos she requested, she said she would have the surgeon look at them and provide his opinion. While I waited nervously, expecting the worst, the waiting room at the hospital continued to fill up. About 30 minutes after sending the photos, I received a message saying that the surgeon was happy to continue with the reassignment surgery as planned, and he would address the other issues when I arrived in Thailand. This was an immense relief to hear. But in the back of my mind, I had my GP's voice echoing her concerns for my health. Based on that, I continued to wait at the hospital. Six and a half hours after arriving, I was called in to see the nurse on duty. After a quick chat with me, they took photos of the issues and showed them to the doctor on duty. On their return, I was informed that there was no one there who could offer any help and that I should go home. What a waste of an afternoon and evening. It was now 10 pm, and I was exhausted. I also knew that I had another big day the following day as it was Saturday, the day of the gala.

The day arrived. The day I would reveal the new me to my friends at the gala event. The day I screamed loudly, I am Carla, look at me. That morning, I slipped my dress on and headed for the salon. My beautician and her team would work their final magic. While I reclined at the washbasin, I felt a wave of euphoria rush over my body. I felt amazing and knew that the team would do their best to make me look amazing. The team took complete control of my look for the day. They spent what felt like an eternity styling my hair. In reality, it was only about an hour. At the end, I emerged with beautiful soft curls. My euphoria levels rose even further. I was feeling beautiful for the first time in my life.

The next stage of my transformation was getting my makeup done. I had never experienced this before, so I was both nervous and excited. What was I going to look like at the end of this? Was I going to look fem or was I going to look like a guy pretending to be a girl? All these thoughts were raging through my head. Quickly, the makeup artist had me at ease, working her magic. The following hour flew past in the blink of an eye. She was done. Now time for the reveal.

Chapter 12

When she held the mirror up, I almost cried. I could not believe what I was seeing. I was looking at the reflection of Carla, and she was happy. I felt complete; I felt whole. I had never felt this feminine in my life. My fears all quickly dissipated and were replaced with euphoria. I am Carla.

That evening, I picked up my bestie, who looked absolutely stunning in her sequin dress, and headed for the event. We were both looking forward to the evening. It was the first evening of this nature that she had been to in a long time, and I felt like it was my big reveal. We were the first of our group to arrive that evening, but as we waited outside, the rest of my Relay family arrived and welcomed me home. I felt amazing as we headed inside and took our seats. One group at the adjoining table dubbed us the sparkly girls. This fed my level of euphoria, which only climbed as the evening went on. For those who know me, know I don't dance, but my bestie got me up that night, and I had a ball. I felt alive. I felt like I had stamped my mark and announced: I have finally arrived; I am enough, and I am loving life.

After the evening ended, a few of us headed into town. This was an eye-opening experience for me. I was used to listening to my female friends remark about the unwanted attention and comments they received when they went out. But as I never took part in this behaviour, it was always at arm's length. Not tonight. Both of us became the subject of many unwanted comments. In reply, I would typically thank them and slide in the words *'If only you knew'*… While these remarks made me feel uncomfortable, they fuelled my euphoria. Not only had I passed as a cisgender female but an attractive one who was catching people's eyes.

Monday was a long day in the tattoo chair while my artist from South Side Tattoo added to my growing art collection. All of my tattoos have a story behind them; they are not random but deeply representative of my story. But on that day, I added two of my most symbolic tattoos. The first was a simple tongue-in-cheek trans rainbow, which flagged my birth year but, more importantly, 2022, the year I established myself. My journey through life has not been straightforward. I had tried to hit the self-destruct button several times and failed. My world was filled with doubt and confusion, but no longer is this the case. From the ashes of who I was, I was rising and becoming my true authentic self. The tattoo artist captured my rising from the ashes as a large phoenix. Every time I get a glimpse in the mirror, it reminds me of where I have been and that I am now rising.

The rest of that week was a blur while I readied myself for the last trip. This time, I was headed to Thailand for what was to be my fourth and final surgery. My surgical journey was coming rapidly to an end.

12 Months

12 months have barely passed

Since the day I took my first step

Time has flown

Life has changed so much

Gone is the façade

I am becoming me

The true me

Who I was born to be

As I take the next step

In this magical journey I am on

My heart races

And the tears flow

I cry both happy and sad

I look at photos

Taken not much more than a year ago

Who is that

I don't recognise the face

Or recall that expression

I wonder who that person was

Looking back at me

That person was me but not the real me

Reality sets in

The past 12 months have flown past

With each memory the smile grows

As I grew and continue to grow

The jet pack equipped snail

Rocketed me from step to step

Testosterone blockers from February 2022

Oestrogen from June 2022

Carla was coming of age

Body feminisation April 2023

Facial feminisation May 2023

Sex reassignment surgery

Now just a few days away

This is the final surgical step

Or is it a giant leap

Chapter 12

My skin suit finally fits

Well almost

Just missing the last bit

I look in the mirror

I see a new face

A face that for once smiles free

I see a new façade

I am me

The true me

As the plane pushes back

I say, see you soon

The last leg of my surgical metamorphosis is upon me

The distinctive smell of jet fuel

Fires up my sensors

The high-pitched whine of the engines

Screams in my ears

Thrust into my seat as the plane accelerates

I am away

Thailand, here I come

My heart and my sole

My mind and my spirit

The scream in unison

This is you

Become you

Own you

I hear these cries

They resonate through my body

I feel the strength they provide

I am me

The true me

I am free

I am at peace

Chapter 13

Thailand Tripping

Beep, beep, beep — what is that sound resonating in my brain? It's 3 am, for goodness' sake! Time to get up as the next leg of this crazy journey I am on was starting. In just over an hour, I was getting picked up and taken to the airport. I was off to Thailand, off to get my last surgery. Ironically, this felt very different from my Argentinian adventure. I was calm and relaxed, yet excited for what was about to happen.

Following a 10-hour flight, the chaos of Thailand greeted me. I couldn't believe how busy the airport was. There were people everywhere, many of whom appeared to be in a mad rush to get to wherever they were headed. After clearing customs, I took the first steps of my Thai adventure, an adventure that would change my life forever. After reaching out to my Becky and Cheery, who would also be my nurses, via messenger, I headed to my pickup point. Once there, I was welcomed with smiles and a hello. I felt instantly at ease with them; I felt safe. These two beautiful humans were going to be looking after me for the duration of my stay.

Once at my accommodation and settled, they wanted to see for themselves the hole in my leg and the incision in my glutes that had haunted me for several months. Both were horrified when they looked at the state of my leg. They were amazed that a surgeon would have left my leg in that state. What made it even worse was when I explained the recommended treatment. All the surgeons in Argentina had given me was a saline spray to clean the area with. What I didn't know was that one of my contacts specialised in wound care and set to work trying to rectify the situation. She started her treatment program of deep cleaning and antiseptic powders. With time, this new treatment strategy worked, and the hole in my leg slowly closed.

A few days after arriving, we battled the Thai traffic and headed to see the surgeon. The trip, while only less than 20km, took well over an hour, even when using the toll roads. The congestion quite took me aback; it was like nothing I had experienced in the past. Not long after arriving at the surgeon's clinic, I was ushered into a consulting room, where I came face to face with the man who would shape my future. I was nervous, as it was still unclear if the surgery would go ahead given the hole in my leg and the issue with the glute implants. Following a detailed review, the surgeon was comfortable that he could operate, but he still wanted to discuss it with the rest of the surgical team. When I left that afternoon, it was unclear whether my Thai adventure was over before it had begun. I was anxious and concerned. Several hours later, my concerns were eased when I received a message to say that the surgery was going ahead as planned. In a few days, my birth defect, as I looked upon my penis, would be rectified. I would be transformed into the woman I always was.

Happy E day. It was June 14, 2023, 12 months after starting my HRT journey. It also marked the day that I was admitted and underwent my surgery. Surgery that I viewed as life-changing and lifesaving. While I was looking forward to the surgery, I was not overjoyed by the pre-surgery preparation. I was introduced to the enema. What a horrible feeling that was. At 4 pm, as planned, I walked through the operating theatre doors and laid down on the surgical table. I took in my surrounds while I waited for the surgery to begin. The size of the team that was present in the theatre amazed me. It felt like there were close to a dozen people in that room. The technology I was surrounded by also amazed me. This was a different theatre from the one I was operated on in Argentina. I remember lying there and having the Monty Python Meaning of Life skit playing through my head. I was wondering if they had the machine that went ping.

The surgeon checked in with me to see if this was really what I wanted to do. He reminded me that it was irreversible, and my life was about to transform. I was at peace with what was about to happen. Not long after chatting with him, the anaesthesiologist placed the gas mask over my face, telling me to breathe deeply. The gas was making me feel sick. Eventually, the lights and sounds faded as I slipped off to sleep. The next thing I remember is waking up in my room the following day. I was told that the surgery went on for almost 12 hours. It was over; I wasn't in any pain, which I was surprised by. I was uncomfortable more than anything else. Even in my groggy state, the euphoric rush had me smiling. I was a new woman. My body now completely matched my soul. Little did I know what was to come.

Early that morning, I had a visit from the doctor and was told that I would have to stay in bed for the next five days. I was instantly uncomfortable with this. How am I going to stay in bed for the next five days when my mind wants me to be doing things every five minutes? What made matters worse was that my room didn't have a window. It felt like I was trapped in a prison cell. My mind was not coping with this scenario and spiralled into negativity. I regretted having the surgery and hated the fact that I was trans. The negativity sucked all my euphoria. I was permanently connected to an IV drip and not allowed any solid food for the duration of the stay. Over the week I dropped 6 kg. The days felt as if they dragged on forever. The lack of a window meant I couldn't tell if it was day or night. It was a horrible experience. I was flat and felt alone, even though I wasn't. But I had my support team back at home keeping me going. I also had an assistant in the room, helping me whenever I needed it. One of the best things she did during this time was give me regular leg and back massages. Those five days tested my resilience in a big way, but I survived them.

I was woken early on day five by the doctor and a team of nurses. They removed the bandages, catheter, and packing. This was the first time that I got to see my designer vagina, as I called it. It wasn't pretty, I can tell you. It was swollen, bloody, and bruised, but it was mine. Whilst there, the doctor dilated me for the first time. This was an uncomfortable experience, but one I would have to get used to. Once he left, I tried to get up to go to the bathroom, but my legs had forgotten how to work after being idle for a week. They were like jelly. When I stood up, they wobbled and buckled underneath me, leading me to fall back into bed. Another half hour passed, and I tried again. This time, my legs held, and with my assistant's help, I made it to the bathroom. On my way out, I got lightheaded; the room spun, and I felt myself collapsing. I reached for the doorframe to help prop me up. My assistant picked up on what was happening and helped me to my bed once the dizzy spell had passed. While I struggled to go to the bathroom, this was an important step towards freedom as I had to use the bathroom several times prior to being discharged. For the next few hours, I pushed myself to get up and stretch my legs and to use the bathroom. I needed to move, and I needed to get out of the hospital.

Not long after ticking the freedom boxes, my Becky and Cheery met me. Seeing their smiling faces enter the room made me smile. I knew I would go back to my apartment soon. I would have my freedom back. After being wheeled to the car, we headed off into the Bangkok traffic. The journey home was an uncomfortable one. All the way home, I constantly wriggled and squirmed while I tried to work out how I could sit without the designer vagina causing me pain. All I wanted to do was lie down and take the pressure off. Yet, when we got to the apartment, the idea of lying down was not appealing. I ignored the discomfort and forced myself to go for a short walk outside in the apartment complex gardens. It felt good to go for the walk, but it took a lot out of me. I spent the rest of that day back in bed.

The following morning, Cheery came to the apartment to start the regular cleaning and dilation routine. Her bedside manner put me at ease. I felt safe and knew that I had the right support at hand. Following the dilation session, I headed outside again, feeling much stronger than the day before. Walking outside, the humidity smacked you in the face. It was horrid, but it was necessary for me to be outside. My mental health was struggling. I was simultaneously euphoric and dysphoric. It was an odd sensation. I was in love with my new body but questioning what I had done. I think the questioning was underpinned by the ongoing maintenance requirements of the designer vagina. This thing was going to be a lot of work, and I was questioning was it was worth it. Deep down, I knew I had done what I needed to do to feel me, the real me.

I was healing well. Although a few days after being released, I started collapsing every time that I got up. I would stand, and the world would spin, my legs would buckle and eventually give way. The next thing I remember is coming to on the floor. Even though I was collapsing, I was not too concerned about it. I would just get up and get on with whatever I was going to do. I didn't give it a second thought. This all changed later that afternoon when I woke up in a pool of blood, and my pyjamas were soaked in blood. I quickly messaged Becky and Cheery, telling them what had happened. Not long after, Cheery arrived and kicked straight into action. She cleaned me up and checked me out. We both breathed a sigh of relief when she said the designer vagina was okay and that the blood had all come from the glute incision site. The following day, I was taken for a blood test and to see the surgeon.

During the surgical consult, I was given two pieces of bad news. The first one was that I needed to go back to the hospital to have blood transfusions. I was so over hospitals. At least the blood transfusion would be given in a hospital rather than my apartment, like they were done in Argentina. The second bit of news was more confronting. The surgeon examined the gluteal incision and the implants. Following his examination, he indicated the implants needed to be removed as one was not in its pocket. That explained why the wound had not healed, and sitting was uncomfortable. In short, the surgeon in Argentina had failed to install the implants properly. I was completely gutted by this news but not overly surprised. After leaving the surgeon's office and on my way to the hospital, I contacted the surgeon in Argentina and explained the situation. The response I got was dismissive, basically telling me there was nothing wrong with the implants. He wiped his hands of it all. His actions left me with very mixed feelings about my Argentinian experience. While I loved the results, I now realised how lax the care had been.

As I walked inside the hospital, I got flashbacks to when I was there a few days earlier. I dreaded being back in a room with no windows. Was it night? Was it a day? This time, I ended up in a room with a window. While I didn't want to be there, at least I could see outside. It was a long night as the

Chapter 13

first transfusion didn't start till almost midnight. The following morning, my levels were checked, but they had not reached the target, so another bag of blood was ordered. My hopes of getting out that morning were dashed. I would spend the best part of the following day hooked up to the infusion. Fortunately, the second infusion just got me above the target level, so I could leave. I was free once more but still felt like I was not running on all cylinders. I was tired and uncomfortable. The black dog raised its head again, causing me to question my decision to undergo sex reassignment surgery and the last few months of my life. Would I ever win this battle, or would the dog keep coming back to bite me? I guess time will tell.

The next week passed relatively quickly. I was back in my normal routine. My nurse would come twice a day, clean my wounds and dilate me. After the morning session, I would typically head to the 7-Eleven shop and get their chocolate signature. While I rarely like chocolate-flavoured drinks, this one was comforting as it had the familiar Milo taste I enjoyed. With a drink in hand, I would sit on the grounds, observing the world passing me by. I found this to be incredibly relaxing, like it reset me. Part of my self-care routine would see me frequent the hairdresser to get my hair washed and blow-dried. These hair washes were the best $15 I ever spent. As I lay with my head in the basin, the hairdresser's magic fingers would melt me into a trance-like state of deep relaxation. After each session, I would leave feeling physically and spiritually refreshed.

Becky and Cheery were both aware of my need to be doing things to maintain my mental health. In the lead-up to what would be my fifth surgery in three months, they took me out on several excursions. One of the first trips out was to a baby expo, as Cheery was seven months pregnant and wanted to buy some baby items. Walking around the expo, I loved watching her eyes light up when she spotted things of interest. It brought back beautiful memories of when my girls entered my life. These memories were a double-edged sword; they cut deep and reminded me that my transition had placed a wedge between my girls and me. Not having them in my life had left a gaping hole that the black dog leveraged and dragged me down. To overcome these emotions, I would remind myself that all I wanted was for the girls to know that they needed to be their true selves and be happy. I would also reflect on the fact that if I hadn't transitioned, I would probably be dead, ending all hope of having them in my life again. I would also leverage the skills I had learnt when I was an inpatient at South Coast Private.

One of my fondest memories from Thailand was going to Ayutthaya, about 80 km from Bangkok. When we got there, we went to an elephant sanctuary, where I got a hug from a

Chapter 13

6-year-old baby elephant and had the chance to ride one that was rescued from a logging camp. Riding an elephant is a bit like sitting on a trotting horse as you rock forward and backwards with each step the elephant takes. The ride took us to a viewing area where we could look over some ruins. While they were impressive, I had not seen the true Ayutthaya.

After a short drive, we arrived at the major site. Cheery and I both battled the heat and went to look at not only the ruins but also the newer Buddhist temple built outside the city walls. From the outside, the temple was a majestic white building, gleaming in the sun. The two large doors at the top of the stairs beckoned you in. Once inside, you were greeted by a large golden Buddha and surrounded by many other smaller sculptures of Buddha. What struck me the most was the instant calmness that swept through me as I crossed the threshold. It was surreal to think that simply entering the temple had such an emotional impact on me.

After exploring the temple, we headed to the ruined city, Ayutthaya, the former capital of Siam. It's at the confluence of three rivers that formed the island on which the city was built. Walking through the city walls, amazing structures constructed from handmade bricks appeared before us. The site comprises several palaces, homes, sun-bleached statues of Buddha, and towering Buddhist temple spires. The architecture draws you in, forcing you to contemplate how such structures were constructed. The craftsmanship was breathtaking. I contemplated how many people had trodden these paths when the city was in its heyday. Walking through the ruins, I was overcome by a feeling of tranquillity; the place felt safe; it felt calming, and healing. This UNESCO World Heritage Site took my breath away.

Later that day, we headed to Becky's sister-in-law's home. This was my first experience of a traditional Thai home. The façade's weatherbeaten teak timbers showed its age, while exuding character. The home was on the bank of a large river and, as such, was built up on stilts. Even though the home sat high above the water, it would often flood. The ladies who lived there even had a small boat tethered to the home at floor level, so when it flooded, they could still get out. Walking up the stairs and into the home, I was forced to duck my head to get under beams and through the door. I guess the home was not designed to accommodate Westerners. Once inside, the space opened into several enormous areas with minimal furnishings. The cavernous interior was cool yet warm and welcoming.

The day arrived when I was back off to the hospital. This time, it was different. I was angry that I was about to have another surgery. The anger was fed from within because I had just wasted a lot of money to have the glute implants put in and now, I was paying for them to be removed because of a surgeon's incompetence. While I was angry, I was relieved as I knew once they were removed, the issues I was having with them should be behind me. That evening, I didn't get any sleep as I waited to be taken to the theatre. One thing I learnt about my Thai surgeon is that he likes to operate at night. At 1 am, I was taken from my room to another waiting area. Another three hours passed before I was taken into the operating theatre. Prior to being sedated, the surgeon told me that once he removed the implants, he would also do a labiaplasty to improve the appearance of my designer vagina. Several hours later, I woke in my room feeling great. I felt I could get out of bed and leave instantly. This was the best I had felt after any of the surgeries I had undergone. I guess this could be because it was the shortest duration surgery I'd had.

Seven days and counting. That's all I had left in Thailand before flying home. I needed to keep busy to keep my mind active. After a few days to recover post-op, Cheery took me out to one of the local malls, where we wandered for the day. While we didn't really look at anything, the simple act of being out was enough to help distract me and reset me. The following day, we headed to another shopping centre, where we again spent the day. We also watched a movie. I really enjoyed spending time with her. Her care of me extended well beyond looking after my wounds.

The following day, I was off to see the surgeon to get my final clearance. The two-hour trip into the office was a real eye-opener. I had never witnessed traffic this heavy. At one stage, we were averaging 100m every five minutes. While we were an hour late getting to the clinic, it was okay as the surgeon was also running late and had not arrived yet. Eventually, he arrived, and I was escorted into the back room, where I was placed in stirrups, and he inspected his handiwork. After the examination, my designer vagina was given the thumbs up. I was cleared to return home and confident knowing that all was well. On the way home from the clinic, emotions overcame me, and I cried. I realised my crazy, intense journey was at an end. I had just undergone five surgeries in two countries in under three months. I was a new woman and felt amazing; I felt complete.

Chapter 13

<u>Five Surgeries</u>

Driving on the crowded streets of Bangkok

Overcome with emotion

The tears began to flow

Tears of happiness

Tears of joy

I realised that my surgical transformation was complete

What a crazy ride

A whirlwind in fact

Five surgeries

Two countries

In less than three months

Something most would do over three years

But dysphoria and the black dog

Drove me on.

The changes have been extreme

Both the physical and the mental

Surgery 1

The body started to take shape

Surgery 2

The face emerged

Surgery 3

The hairline was fixed

Surgery 4

PPV to complete the transformation

Surgery 5

A revision from surgery 1

A set back

But not a game changer

I look in the mirror

And see my new face

I see my new body

I feel my heart beating as one

My soul is at rest

Inner peace descends

My body and mind now merge

They march to the beat of the same drum

Chapter 13

I am the woman

The woman I had always been

Gone was the façade

The real me had emerged

Like a butterfly from its chrysalis

Time to spread the magic

I stretched my wings

It's time to fly

Now fly

Arriving at the airport was tough. When I got out of the car, the tears began welling in my eyes. The journey was at an end. I had been blessed to have Becky and Cheery by my side for this last phase of the surgical journey. While they drove off, the tears continued to roll down my face like raindrops on a window. My life had changed forever, and these people had been there holding my hand, holding my heart, and caring for me. I will always treasure the time I shared with them. They had become members of my extended family, my chosen family.

Chapter 14

Battling the Black Dog

I have made no secret throughout this book that I have struggled with mental health. My struggles started at an early age and were in full force by the time I was in my teens. During these early years, I turned to alcohol, high-risk activities, and self-harm. None of these was a great idea, nor did it fix the issues. They simply masked the pain, the internal anguish. I was essentially on self-destruct mode. Blindly fumbling my way through life.

What underpinned this pain was never clear-cut in the early years. I had too much going on in my world simultaneously. I was dealing with childhood trauma, which came with a heavy dose of pain and guilt. I was growing up in a house at war, with two parents who clashed regularly. Even at school, there was no respite. I was being bullied daily. Life was miserable and lonely.

While all of this was going on, I didn't realise what the black dog was really biting my heels about. This was a subconscious black dog, a dog I could not see or hear. How do you fight something that you don't even know is there?

Chapter 14

It's only now that I realise, as I'm taking the time to reflect on my life, that the unseen dog was gender dysphoria. I was not comfortable in my skin. I was not the boy that I was raised to be. I was a scared little girl trapped in a boy's body and a boy's world.

Over the years, I was in and out of psychologists. While they all tried to help, none of them could help me fight the black dog. The black dog's grip on my psyche only got stronger as the years passed. I continued implementing my maladaptive coping strategies. The drinking became more frequent, the risks I took more extreme, and the self-harm more frequent. In my late teens, turning to the gym became a positive feedback loop. I played over and over in my head, 'You're not good enough'. I was losing the fight. The black dog was all-consuming.

During my marriage, there were glimpses of hope. There were moments when it looked like I was winning the battle. The reality was life was simply so busy that I lost sight of the dog. It was there, hiding in the background. It was big, black and mean. Failing to recognise this and the circumstances that I was living in were only feeding the dog. It was being nourished in secret. Growing stronger by the day.

Reality bit hard on the Central Australia trip. My eyes were pried open as I took in the vastness of my happy place. I had regained my sight; I could again see and feel the black dog. It was huge and scary. It was relentless and vicious. But I knew it was there. If I could see it, I fought it. Maybe now it would be a fair fight. One I could win. One I must win, or it would kill me.

Once home from the trip, the unpacking began. During this unpacking phase, the precursor to this book was written. As the words appeared on the page, it was like peeling back the layers of an onion. It was just a large onion with many layers. While onions are ultimately sweet to eat, the amino acids that form a type of sulfuric acid (lachrymator) can cause tears. I, too, cried many tears as I peeled my onion. They were tears of happiness and tears of sadness, loss, and guilt. I was happy that I could now see but saddened by what I saw. This was the moment I realised the odds had finally swung my way.

With the blindfold removed, my medical team got to meet me — the real me. They were now in a better position to help me unpack my world and provide me with the tools to move forward and live a full life, my best life. One thing I remember fondly was when my psychologist said to me, *"Nice to meet you."* These simple words made me smile. They made me realise I had not been open. The deeper we dove, the more complex things became, but my medical team held my hand. I realised how much I was dealing with. No wonder I was turning a blind eye to the black dog. Avoidance had become my thing.

Chapter 14

I always hated being labelled. But I realised that sometimes labels are needed so that we can be healed. In the past, I was unofficially diagnosed with ASD 1 (Autism Spectrum Disorder) or high-functioning autism. This diagnosis explained a lot of my behavioural traits. My need for order, difficulty in adjusting to change, difficulty in reading body language and my typically black and white view of the world.

As my psychological team dived deeper unpacking my past, they both landed on Complex Post-Traumatic Stress Disorder (CPTSD), Borderline Personality Disorder (BPD) and Attention-Deficit Hyperactivity Disorder (ADHD). CPTSD is like the more well-known Post Traumatic Stress Disorder (PTSD). The fundamental difference is that CPTSD results from multiple traumas over an extended period, often during childhood.

For me, CPTSD manifests in a range of ways. One of the earliest signs related to the recurring flashbacks to the abuse. These would often happen at night as I was trying to go to sleep. I could replay with clarity the events of one particular evening in which the most complex and perverse abuse occurred. The replaying of these moments fuels feelings of shame, disgust, and guilt, which drive my depression and lack of self-worth. CPTSD also impacts my ability to form meaningful relationships across a wide range of scenarios and difficulty with emotional regulation. All these factors can hamper my daily functionality. Some days, the impact is negligible, and I can appear to be fully functional. On other days, I just want to crawl into a ball and hide as I often become a sledgehammer when communicating with people, becoming very black and white.

While CPTSD and BPD are very similar to each other, the primary difference is that BPD is believed to be genetic, essentially hardwired. While it is hardwired, not everyone who is coded that way will develop the disorder. Researchers believe that those who display BPD symptoms have had environmental factors trigger its onset. Neurologically, BPD results from neurotransmitters malfunctioning, sending improper messages to the brain. It's also driven by under-or overactive parts of the brain, including the amygdala, hippocampus, and orbital frontal cortex, which regulate emotions, control behaviour, and process or decide.

While many of the symptoms are common between CPTSD and BPD, there are several key differences. For me, the BPD manifests as intense negative emotions, mood swings, suicidality, poor self-perception, self-harm, intense conversations with myself, engaging in high-risk activities and, to a degree, unstable relationships. The plus side of the BPD diagnosis is that I now take medication to help regulate the symptoms. While the medication is no silver bullet, it has definitely helped me to regulate and improve my ability to function daily. They are helping me to fight the black dog.

Like my ASD diagnosis, the ADHD diagnosis needs to be explored further. The complexity of my mental health and the events that have driven it, as stated above, manifests. Cognitive and mood factors underpin the ADHD diagnosis. From a cognitive perspective, I can have difficulty focusing, forgetfulness, problems paying attention. From a mood perspective, the key symptoms include anxiety, boredom, low frustration tolerance, trouble managing stress and mood swings. There is significant crossover in symptoms between the various diagnoses. This makes landing on a final position very challenging. Irrespective of whether other labels are accurate, I am who I am, and I have the associated challenges to manage daily.

Since starting my transition and journey to being the real me, loneliness and guilt have plagued me. They both feel like massive weights pressing down on my shoulders, driving me into the ground. These emotions have been fuelling the black dog of late and placing me on an emotional rollercoaster. Typically, throughout the day, I can emotionally regulate myself as I keep busy mostly. This is a classic avoidance. At night, when I am sitting at home on my own, is when the black dog bites. The sound of silence results in rumination and feelings of loss and guilt kicking in. All thoughts of self-compassion are parked, and the storytelling begins. These moments often lead to my spiralling and resorting to old habits.

Alcohol drowns my sorrows, but it only hydrates the dog. It becomes a vicious cycle until I crash. I will admit there have been days when suicidal thoughts have been very strong. I have even gone as far as tying the noose that would end it all. The scariest thing is that I have no real recollection of those events. I can't remember tying the rope or that I posted saying goodbye. I remember being placed in an ambulance by police and then being taken to hospital, where I was involuntarily admitted under the Mental Health Act. Disassociation of mind and body is a curse. I often just want the pain to end. But how do you stop the pain when you don't know you're in pain? While these dark moments creep in, I am now more aware and able to catch them. I hope with time, my capacity to fight strengthens, and I'm able to catch the slide before it begins.

Reaching out to my medical team and my friends has saved my life. If I had not opened up to them as I have been doing, they, like others in the past, would not have been able to help me. But now I have a team helping me, coaching me on how to fight the black dog, and with time and the continued support of these people, I feel I can win the fight. I know I will always have to manage the dog, but hopefully, I can muzzle it and put it on a short lead. I will take control, not the other way around.

Black Dog

The black dog bites down

Teeth sink deep into my skin

They penetrate my soul

They pierce my mind

My thoughts are clouded

I have named my dog

I call it Solo

For I am alone with my thoughts

I am alone in this place I now call home

Yet I am at peace with who I am

Why do I feel this way?

As I sit and watch the light of the day fade

That black dog becomes more aggressive

It manipulates my mind

Brings my fears to the fore

And tears came to my eyes

Eyes open is not something that sits easily
Eyes closed and descended into darkness
The curtain of the dark envelopes me
Like the blackness of the deepest cave
At times this feels like my only choice

I try to fight the dog
With the skills I have been taught
But these skills don't always work
These skills only take me so far
I need to fight the dog
I need to win
I will win

Chapter 14

I have spent much of life loathing the person who I was. One of my greatest accomplishments in fighting the dog is that I am learning to love myself. This newfound love is multifaceted. My battle with dysphoria has been won. I am now the woman that I always was. I am a female with a trans past. The second factor relates to the group therapy sessions at South Coast Private that I have been attending twice a week. These sessions have been teaching me the skills I need to not only survive but to thrive. I discovered that the guilt I felt towards the girls because of my transition was misplaced, as I did not go on this journey intending to hurt anyone. I went on this journey to find and heal myself. Understanding and accepting this has unloaded a significant metaphorical weight that was holding me back. Don't get me wrong, I am saddened by the impact my transition has had on my girls. But I feel that having a parent live by their values, be the best they can be, and be their true and authentic self, is important and a positive thing.

<u>Learning to Love</u>

Dysphoria controls my mind

My skin crawls

The discomfort

The unpleasantness

This skin suit doesn't fit

My mind and soul are at war

Three countries

Six surgeries later

My skin suit finally fits

My mind has raced to catch up

My thoughts rolled and tumbled

Like tumbleweed rolling across the plains

I need to learn

I need to grow

As I wipe away my tears

I reveal a new me

My skin no longer crawls

The discomfort and unpleasantness are no more

The smile begins to return

I'm learning to love myself

The guilt I feel is heavy

It weighs me down

Bogging my thoughts

Making my heart heavy

But as I sit and breathe

The weight begins to lift

I'm learning to love myself

On my own

While surrounded by people

I feel alone in this world

The world I am building

I mindfully sit with this feeling

I self-soothe

Comforting, calming and relieving

I find the middle ground

Treat myself kindly

I'm learning to love myself

I accept these feelings

I sit with the discomfort of them

I accept that I am human

And painful experiences will occur

I greet them with open arms

I greet them with self-compassion

They no longer control me

I befriend them

They have their own dignity

I am learning to love me

No longer at war

My shell, heart and soul now aligned

I walk this world as my authentic self

The real me for all to see

My strength has returned

I am resilient

I have survived and dropped the struggle

Now, I'm learning to love me

Chapter 14

You may wonder why I am sharing this information and what relevance it has. It has everything to do with my journey; it defines who I am today and will shape my future. Also, many of the symptoms I face are shared with others in the transgender community, my community. I share this information hoping it may help just one person who reads these words. I hope it may take a step towards normalising the fight, and that it is okay not to be okay. I also hope that sharing the information about my diagnosis, and the various ways that it manifests may help others to accept their symptoms and see that there is hope.

Chapter 15

Freedom

∞

The last two years of my life have been frenetic, at best. A lot has changed, both physically and mentally. I am not the same person who I was just a short time ago. When I started this journey of self-discovery, self-doubt, sadness, and loneliness plagued me. Now, I have found freedom.

Although I initially resisted going to South Coast Private, I now look at it through a different lens. I now see that my time at the hospital as an inpatient was exactly what I needed. However, my greatest growth has occurred as an outpatient. Every Monday and Thursday, I returned to the hospital for my group therapy sessions. Taking part in these groups is where I learnt to love myself, among other things. The group environment was a safe space. We share our stories, exposing our soft underbellies. We supported each other and encouraged each other. We grew together. While our stories are all different, a common thread binds us together. We are striving for freedom from the black dog.

Reflecting on my past, I can see that I was lacking the role models needed in my life to build my healthy adult. I grew up in an environment that fostered my demanding and punitive parent schemas. My inner critic was strong. It was now time for me to re-parent, with the help of others. I had to learn and reprogram my subconscious mind. Over the months that I participated in the group sessions, I allowed myself the space I needed to heal and start the reprogramming. I provided the space my healthy adult needed to grow. I let myself tell my vulnerable child that they are safe. I uttered words of reassurance, support, and understanding. If I could, I would reach out and hug my child self and tell them that *"One day, you will get to be your true authentic self. You will live your truth. The subconscious torture will eventually end."*

One of my biggest life handbrakes is the view that I'm not good enough. This view has driven me to succeed academically and achieve many things in life. It has driven the perfectionist in me. But it has meant my life has been built on unstable foundations. Foundations that shake uncontrollably with the slightest push.

Every Monday, my mind was forced to focus on learning to be self-compassionate. Self-compassion, although it may sound fluffy, is about treating yourself with kindness, love, and support. It's about filling your own cup in the same way you would fill a friend's or loved one's cup. It's about learning to love yourself. It's about responding to life struggles with kindness.

My self-compassion journey has been enlightening. I have seen even further behind the facade. I have realised that I have been punishing myself for things I can't control, such as the guilt I felt over the impact my transition has had on my two girls. I no longer feel this guilt. I think that living my truth is one of the greatest gifts I can give them. They deserve the true me, and I deserve to be my true self.

My Thursday mornings were occupied with the Acceptance Commitment Therapy (ACT) Masterclass. I went into this class with my eyes half closed. I was sceptical about this class. It all seemed too theoretical and fluffy for my liking. I think I even put a few bricks back in my wall and hid again.

As the weeks passed, the weight lifted off my shoulders. ACT was helping. I was becoming free. I learnt to accept the struggles in my life and realise that I'm human and doing the best I can. Pure awareness descended. I learnt to be mindful and self-soothe. I'm living for today, so I stopped looking over my shoulder and being triggered by my past. I built psychological flexibility and lived by my values.

An amazing lady, who held our hands and took our hearts, facilitated my ACT group. She nurtured our souls. She quickly removed the bricks I had added to my facade when I started. She helped me smash more of that facade. As I think about her, the tears flow. She is an amazing lady who will never truly know the impact she has had on my life.

Chapter 15

While learning about myself in the groups, I formed close bonds with several participants. They accepted me for myself. These people helped me and encouraged me to be me, my true authentic self. I will cherish these friendships.

Taking part in these groups filled my spoon drawer back up. I could deal with life more easily than I had historically. I was free to re-engage with things I loved, like Lego, cycling, and paddling. While death-scrolling on Facebook, I came across a post on the Wild Women of Wollongong page. A member of the Fire Island Outrigger Canoe Club (FIOCC) was seeking expressions of interest from women who were interested in trying paddling. After a few messages, I committed to trying it out on a Saturday morning.

Saturday arrived, and I rolled out of bed. Anxiously, I headed for the harbour where this new adventure was to begin. On arrival, I was introduced to three women, who were also going to try paddling that day. Instantly, we clicked as we chatted nervously together. After the initial briefing, we hit the water.

Splash, splash, splash. We slowly pulled away from the shore. The sound of paddles occasionally broke the splash of the water clashing. The canoe was pulsating back and forward as we were out of time, but this was to be expected, as it was our first time. By the end of the session, we had clicked and were making progress. I was hooked. I had remembered how much I loved being on the water and paddling.

A few days later, I joined in on a morning training session. I was put in a canoe with an experienced crew. I was the odd one out but felt supported by the other five. We headed out of the harbour and into open water. The canoe pitched, rose, and fell as it created the swell. I was in love. My new obsession.

At my third training session, I borrowed a paddle from a senior member of the club. It was a hybrid Pala Famala. I held the paddle and stroked away; I felt at one with it. I needed to get myself one. I found the manufacturer in Hawaii and ordered one. I was surprised at how quickly the paddle arrived. It was in my hands and the water a few days later. What I didn't realise, I was paddling with the Rolls Royce of paddles. In hindsight, I shouldn't have been surprised, as I gravitate toward quality and expensive items.

The newly formed friendships blossomed. We all were having a ball. Not long after coming together, the girls and I started talking about the possibility of forming a team and racing together. Jokingly, we started calling ourselves the 'Old Ducks.' The more time we spent together, the more alike we realised we were. Our friendship was blossoming. I was amazed at how quickly a group of strangers had bonded. Not one of them cared about my past. They saw only Carla. I was becoming increasingly free.

Freedom

The waters lap at my feat

With the gentle sounds of the swish swash

My eyes are drawn to the horizon

They carry my thoughts

Thoughts of freedom

Thoughts of being at one

I push out the canoe

And begin to paddle

An instant calm descends

The silence is deafening

Only broken by the sound of the paddle penetrating deep into the water

Splash, splash, splash

Pulling further from the shore

Pulling further from my old self

I defuse from my thoughts

They are free to be

My thoughts become centred

Pure awareness develops
I am stronger than I ever was
Mindfully I paddle to freedom

At one with the ocean
The rising sun glistens on the water
The warmth of its rays
Penetrate warming my heart and soul
Its light guides my path
I commit to my actions
Every stroke takes me closer
Closer to my values
Closer to my authentic self
The real me is being freed

Escaping the cage
A cage, which has trapped me for years
The openness of the ocean
Draws the weight off my shoulders
Free of the historical burden
I spread my wings and glide
Glide like the sea birds riding the thermal currents
Freedom to be me

Chapter 15

With time, our conversation around competing together became more serious. We started to set ourselves goals. We aimed to prepare and race in Newcastle, just three months after coming together. While we laughed at the 'Old Ducks' name, we started to think about a more serious name. It didn't take long, and we had a few suggestions on the table. Of these suggestions we chose to go with Wild Wahine Koa. When translated, it means Wild Women Warriors.

As a team, we were strong, but I wanted to be stronger. I wanted to spend more time on the water than I could as part of the training sessions. I had often thought about buying myself a sea kayak so I could go paddling. But I had never followed through on this impulse. Things were different. I decided I was going to get myself a kayak or canoe so I could be on the water more often. But which way to go?

The joys of autism and ADHD. I decided and started looking for a second-hand OC1, a single-seat outrigger canoe. Within a few days of deciding, I located one that sparked my interest. It was a Kamanu Composite Pueo. Like the paddle, I had apparently fallen in love with one of the best canoes on the market. I don't know how I keep finding the most expensive stuff. Irrespective of everything, the deal was done, and I now owned an OC1.

Within 24 hours of collecting the OC1, I had it on the water. It was a steep learning curve as this thing wanted to huli (capsize) with the slightest shift of weight in the wrong direction. Within the first hour, I hulied three times. After these initial hulis, it started clicking, and I progressively picked up my pace and stayed upright. I loved the experience and freedom that the OC1 offered. To this day, I paddle it almost every day, when the weather allows. While my paddling journey has just begun, I feel at one with the water. I feel welcomed and supported by the club and my new friends. Most importantly, I feel free.

As 2023 ended, I sat and reflected on the past few years. Particularly in the last 18 months. My world has shifted. My story evolved. I have experienced euphoric highs and the darkest of dark days. But I survived and look forward to what is coming.

2023

At a frantic pace,
The year has passed
A new life begun
A year that I nearly ended it all
At peace but at war

As I reflect, a lot has happened
2023, a year of change
Three countries
Three months
Six surgeries
A new name
A new yet old gender
A new home where I am alone
My brain struggles to process
All that has laid before me

The silence of the day is deafening
No voices other than those in my mind
If it wasn't for my furry friend
Those voices would take me to a dark place
A place I have been before
A place I don't want to go again

2023, a year of tears
A year of fighting to survive
As I discovered who I am
New friendships were forged
Old ones strengthened

2023, a year of hope
For a year, I have survived
A year of growth
Slowly winning the war
Fighting back against the black dog
Self-discovery
Connection with my true identity

2023 will be forever a defining year
A pivotal point in my life
The river of life flowed fast and free
It was a year of me
The raw exposed me
My truth evolved

Chapter 16

The Story Goes On

---∞---

As I write this final chapter, the tears flow freely. The journey that transgender people embark on is highly personal. Yet, one thing that we all share is that the journey is not an easy one. We all face challenges and hurdles. I wrote this book hoping the story shared in its pages will touch someone. The words will hopefully make someone else's life a little easier.

You may wonder why parts of the story are repeated in different ways. This is a deliberate choice as it emphasises that many transgender people continuously have to reinvent themselves. They often must retell their story many times over. It also stands for the complexity of life and the fact that many parts of our life reoccur. Life is not linear.

Writing this book has been a cathartic experience. Getting my story out has helped me to heal. It has helped me to understand where I have come from and to see where my future lies. There are many pages in this story yet to be written. I have only just started my current journey. Life goes on, I will go on. The rest of the story is yet to be written; …

Behind the Façade

Welcome to the world; a baby boy is born

Born of a lesbian mother and a present yet absent father

Born into a house at war, a house that was on the verge of destruction

A volatile world. A world I could not control

I was just a child

Brick by brick

I built a façade

A façade that hid a secret

It hid pain and confusion

It hid a story of abuse

Abuse at the hands of a carer, an educator, a family friend, and a parent

By 13, solace was found in a bottle of spirits

By 15, the scars of time were etched deeply into my skin

By 17, education had been cast aside

By 19, I felt alone

By 21, I had wished for death, but death had not come

Chapter 16

By 23, I had met the person I would marry
The person who I thought provided stability in my life
The person who would become the mother of my two girls
My reasons for living
But life was not as it seemed
The life I had wished for was not real
It was a life where abuse was a regular occurrence
But I hid behind my façade and tried to protect my girls

The gym became my home
Lifting heavier and heavier, but it was never enough
Why was I never strong enough?
Why was I never big enough?
Why did I despise the person I was?
Why was I so uncomfortable in my skin?
Why did I wish for it to end?

Fighting the black dog became increasingly harder
The world around me spiralled out of control
I sat at my desk with a knife holding my head up
My hand firmly on the self-destruct button
While the façade held, it was cracking
How much more could it sustain?

Kati Thanda is a magical place

A place where your eyes are drawn towards the horizon

A place where the blue sky kisses the glistening white salt crust

A place that makes you stop and reflect

A place that made me realise I was hiding behind a façade

Brick by brick

The façade started to come down

The person the world knew was not real

The person was simply a shell

Who is hiding behind the façade?

So many questions and so few answers

As the façade crumbled

I could see a light through the window of life

A light which, while only small and a long way off, shone bright

A light that was guiding me on a new path

A path I never realised was there. but explained so many things

A path painted white, pink, and blue

Chapter 16

The façade is down

The remains lay scattered around me

The boy who was born all those years ago

The boy who has struggled to survive

The boy who built a façade to hide behind

The boy who became a man…

Was always a woman

I have found who is hiding behind the façade

I have found a person who wants to embrace what life has to offer

I have found a person who is stronger than they have ever been

I have found a person who is truly happy

My heart and mind are now at peace

I am now free to spread my wings and fly

About the Author

Carla's story is one of relentless reinvention and intellectual curiosity. From humble beginnings as a high school dropout, Carla carved a path that defies convention and inspires awe. Today, Carla holds an extraordinary seven academic diplomas and degrees, including a PhD in Science, each one a testament to her insatiable thirst for knowledge and her refusal to be boxed in.

Her professional journey is as diverse as her academic one. Carla began her career in the mining industry, working as a mechanic—hands-on, gritty, and grounded. She later transitioned into engineering, specialising in the environmental performance of buildings, where she combined technical precision with a passion for sustainability. Now, she's channelling her deep understanding of systems—both mechanical and ecological—into the human psyche, working toward becoming a registered psychologist.

Carla is a conversational chameleon: equally at ease discussing quantum physics or the nuances of emotional resilience, she brings warmth, wit, and wisdom to every exchange. Whether the topic is light and playful or deeply introspective, Carla's presence invites connection and reflection.

Her life is a living example of metamorphosis—proof that transformation is not only possible, but powerful.

Live your truth.

Copyright © 2026 Carla Hope

www.ingramcontent.com/pod-product-compliance
Lightning Source LLC
Chambersburg PA
CBHW061725070526
44583CB00024B/3014